BDG
DIARIES
Learn-n-Intern

BIKRAM DASGUPTA

RUPA

Published by
Rupa Publications India Pvt. Ltd 2022
7/16, Ansari Road, Daryaganj
New Delhi 110002

Sales Centres:
Allahabad Bengaluru Chennai
Hyderabad Jaipur Kathmandu
Kolkata Mumbai

P-ISBN: 978-93-5520-890-3
E-ISBN: 978-93-5520-891-0

First impression 2022

10 9 8 7 6 5 4 3 2 1

Printed in India

To my life partner Babli (Ranjana), as we call her,
who has been with me in every
part of this exciting journey and has actively
played her role in it.

Thank you Babli for being there.

CONTENTS

SECTION THREE
MIDDLE-CLASS DILEMMA

SECTION FOUR
COVID-19 TEACHINGS

PREFACE

I started writing blogs (renamed as 'Short Stories') rather by accident. After handing over the business to my sons, I had a lot of space and time on my hands.

I realised, and I confess, that I was a highly 'episodic', action-oriented person and my complete focus was on what I was doing at that point in time. The good news is that I could do a lot because of this. The not-so-good-news is that it took a while for my peers, colleagues and the public at large to really know me and understand what I was doing.

The transition brought in a void. So, I started travelling to Bhutan in search of myself, trying to understand my inner being. Who is Bikram? Who is BDG? And that is what led to these blogs. Whatever came to my mind or was bothering me, or whatever I was going through, I started writing them instantly. However, initially I did not have a platform to share them. All my blogs/short stories contain instant and fresh thoughts that reflect my personal views.

I then wanted to share these thoughts with my young and aspiring friends; so, I started putting all my thoughts and views together and that is how the *BDG Diaries: Learn-n-Intern* happened. Over the years, thousands of youths from the Globsyn fraternity have gone through my L-n-I sessions and this book is also aimed at them—the high-growth aspiring individuals within the age group of 21-35 years.

Thanks to the BDG FireBrand team that was created recently. The team members have been with me through thick and thin. I would like to thank Sharon, Prasanta, Oindrila, Supratik, Saheli, Dhananjay and all others who made this happen. A big thanks to the team for helping me reach out to a wide audience, including students, youngsters, and aspiring men and women.

PROLOGUE

Long, long ago, in the days of communist Bengal, there lived a young man who studied in IIT (Indian Institute of Technology), one of the premier institutions of the country, just for the love of learning. That love for going beyond time and space by exciting the little, grey cells led him to become one of India's leading tech entrepreneurs during an era when India did not even know what information technology was all about. From the first 'Smart Building' of India to the first Tech Finishing School, from the first AI (Artificial Intelligence) generated tech business empire to motivating youths to give back to the society through philanthropy, this man did everything far ahead of his time. Yet, he let his mind and soul wander amidst clouds, seeking spiritual bliss and challenging the dilemmas of the middle-class society in which he was born and bred. He is none other than Bikram Dasgupta who still believes that an entrepreneur's journey never ends, it continues even after his or her 'physical' death.

An entrepreneur thinks beyond what others get to see or understand. Hence 'BDG', as Dasgupta is fondly called by his friends and colleagues, keeps learning, sets his own rules and conquers the fear of failure by facing challenges. This attitude has led him to the pinnacles of success, where even the sky is not the limit. Global IT entrepreneur Bikram Dasgupta has experienced, imbibed and touched upon life's various facets in his 40 years of journey as one of the most successful 'Tech Guru', entrepreneur, investor and philanthropist in India, and a global leader. Through his real-life experiences he has influenced several young minds, and this 'Blog Book with a difference' will enrich hundreds more! Join him in this journey and experience the joy of living and learning!

Young Managers Ahoy!
Hey young manager, are you stressed? Come discover with me the fun of unlearning
??

SECTION ONE

YOUNG MANAGERS AHOY!

AMBIGUITY, THY NAME IS ENIGMA!

'Sorry, I didn't think of it THAT way...' For me ambiguity is always enigma. All plausible interpretations are highly welcome—the more, the merrier. So how do you look at it? Is it a stimulus, a neutral learning curve or a threat? Living in ambiguity gives us all an additional space to manoeuvre. It could be this or that, it could be right or wrong; you could be thinking that the matter is resolved, but I know it hasn't; purely interpretation-based decisions can be taken to suit us and interestingly enough, you can even say, at the end of it all, 'Sorry, I didn't think of it THAT way.'

Our relationships—personal, professional, emotional, legal, or political—may evolve around AMBIGUITY. It has a huge ability to be tolerant, also known as the 'Tolerance of Ambiguity' factor, or TOA, in work life. It may live on for years; however, if you wish you learn from it. Take for example the geopolitical scenario in our borders. Whether it is the LOC (Line of Control) or LAC (Line of Actual Control), both remain unresolved for years. Yet life goes on as usual until we get into a confrontational situation, like what we have now. Then, almost suddenly, both sides wake up and start having discussions on 'Your territory, my territory'. Interesting!

Just the same happens in our professional and personal lives. We hate to resolve our issues because we might find it convenient not to find a solution. People who stick their neck out and say 'Let's resolve', are termed novices, immature, emotional and inexperienced. If you look at our corporate legal system, you will find a similar situation. A lot of the disputes arise because of the different interpretations of law; they live on and get resolved by interpreting the law. Now take a break and look within. Even in our personal, emotional space, ambiguity survives in its enigmatic whole. Relationships, when they end or turn sour, become hugely interpretation-based, and remain in the domain of ambiguity, with both sides feeling the same way about being right or wrong.

This will perhaps remain. We will need to accept it as a way of life. We need to be alert, or savvy, as the case maybe, to deal with our personal, professional and institutional issues, where there is ambiguity, and we are required to demonstrate our Tolerance of Ambiguity or the TOA factor.

NEVER GIVE UP!

The death of a well-known Bollywood hero had recently provoked strong reactions, comments, views and allegations. It happened on 14 June 2020—a promising, pleasing, extremely talented and intelligent actor, with multiple facets, took the unfortunate decision to end his life. There is no denying that this is truly a very shocking incident. I remember his acting from a soft family TV Serial where I thought he was pretty impressive.

But let us delve deep, deeper than the chronology of the sad incident. I have been a self-made entrepreneur, first generation, boot-strapped in the technology space for over 30 years now and I feel that this phenomena is prevalent in every sphere of our lives and in every profession. If you are a startup, fledgling and trying to make a mark for yourself, with your innovative products and services, serving the society and bridging the gap through your innovations, then you are sure to face huge challenges.

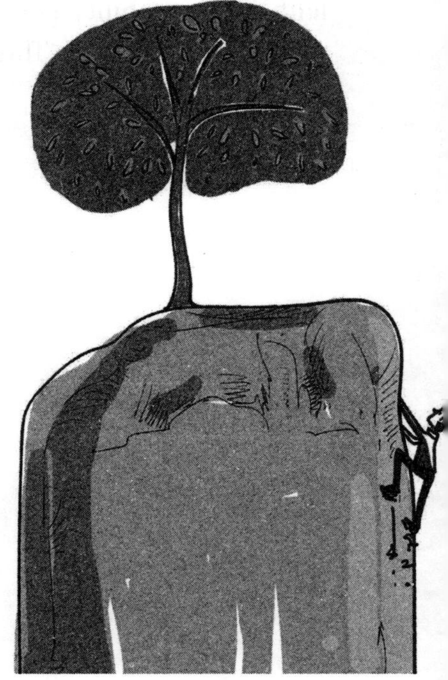

We infer quickly that it is a financial issue, a cash flow issue, but we know deep down that unless an entrepreneur has a family business background, it is tough to survive in this combative world. For here, you are competing with the most resourceful people in the industry who will attempt to crush you as their existence gets threatened due to your ideas and talent. Because you are here to compete and grow, they are frightened of you—the new power. It's a typical David vs Goliath story. It happens very regularly in the industry. So, the startup entrepreneur has very few things up his armory and the primary tool is his own conviction about his products and services, as he is willing to bite the dust till his business ideas succeed and take a definite form. Very tough, but definitely possible.

It has happened to me too. At times it is pretty bad, and you keep looking up at God and asking him: 'Why me?' There are days when you sleep with your issues, almost never to get up again. But again, there comes another day. This journey is arduous, which is why entrepreneurs are comparatively quicker than others to get into social work. That is why meditation becomes such a key tool for all of us—as we would like to go away for a while, to find solace within ourselves. While all this happens, you are also continuously driven by your innovative ideas, financial expansion and growth as they are all part and parcel of your being. Your own conviction, trust and faith in your ability goes through severe tests under such adverse emotional situations. This happens to most of us. There are people who succumb as well.

BE THE WATCHDOG, NOT THE RUMOUR-MONGER

In an entrepreneur's life, especially during the startup phase, when his earnings are less than his expenses, payment of salaries to his employees, and that too on time, has always been a discussion point. Many of these discussions, unfortunately, do not show the true picture of an organisation or its owner, but some of them (as it turns to be) do make for a good 'coffee shop' discussion for job seekers. However, with the advent of social media and the subsequent no-holds-bar communication, the entrepreneur is being hit where it hurts. To some who want to score points with their erstwhile sensitive entrepreneur, this could be a moot point—to score. But for a sensitive entrepreneur who is building an organisation, the payment of salaries to his employees is a matter of pride. He is very proud of the fact the he is, in some ways, responsible for the running of so many families, having provided employment to many. As a first-generation entrepreneur from decades ago, I too have retained this pride as much as possible.

In my case, in the early days, cash flow was always a problem, but not salary. I had observed a simple policy that payment of salaries is linked to the product we sell or the services we offer to our clients, so it is mandatory. I remember those days, when the payment of our salaries totally depended on month-end collections, and paying salary on the 1st of every month always put me in a tight situation. So, I took a decision—that our salaries would be in the bank on the 5th of every month for employees. Yes, the first month was somewhat of an issue for four days, but I addressed an all-employee meeting to tell them why I was doing it.

Everyone instantly agreed to what I had proposed. From that day onwards, our salaries were paid on the 5th of every month, with our collection cycle ending on the 31st of the last month.

Now, of course, with the growth of the enterprise, this is not that relevant, as collections are not always linked to salary payment. Yet, it has shaped the culture in all our companies. An organisation runs on its culture and this is one such thing. But the question is: Have we ever failed to pay our salaries on the 5th as promised? If we have, how did we handle it?

The answer is: Yes. We have failed on two or three occasions. Every time I failed, for reasons beyond my control, I used to write a note to the employees, apologizing for the delay and giving them a date by when they could expect their dues, which would be two or three days later. Again, this sets a culture and defines the importance the organisation gives to such issues. Problems arise due to such issues, due to lack of clarity in communicating effectively. If communication is part of the culture of the organisation, employees mostly respond positively. Such issues came up some 15+ years ago. Now, it is no longer relevant to me.

But I wanted to raise this issue, for there are people who raise such issues during loose interactions, over a cup of coffee, and try mudslinging against an organisation or its culture. I always tell everyone that if anyone faces such issues, please substantiate it with data and make a complaint, and not be a gossip-monger. An entrepreneur's life is difficult. He spends many sleepless nights to build for the society and for himself, something he wants to be proud of. Give him that time. Be a bit kinder to such entrepreneurs who are sensitive, innovative and genuinely trying to contribute to their employees' lives and the overall society. Pulling them down casually may hurt or impact their journey. Be the watchdog, not the rumour-monger.

LISTEN TO PEOPLE

Life takes many twists and turns along its journey. Every now and then we find sunshine on our tracks, or at times there are misty clouds enveloping our senses. But give enough attention to each and every change, however silent they might be. Do we listen to all the inputs we get from our near and dear ones and act on them? Or do we brush them aside, without realising how important their feedback is, particularly for the person who was giving us that feedback.

Trust me, life turns a lot easier when we 'listen'. Once we practice that, understanding people who matter to us becomes easier and the data within our system gets reflected through better decisions. I have realised that throughout my life there have been events that appeared common, simple and unimportant. We often don't give the required attention to an information, or the person who is giving the information. To the person giving the information, it is very important. In the process, we fail to fill the communication gap between two persons. It is only through understanding that we build love and care. Being sensitive to the people you care for, or you think you care for, is quite critical. That itself bridges a lot of gaps between people.

But more often than not, we

try to exercise control through our emotional bonding and need. It might work for a while, but it doesn't last long. Thus, the basic objective is lost. That creates a psychological gap between two people and it may last forever, if not mended. This is sad, but true. So, precise and direct communication between two persons who love and care for each other is a must, especially to reduce gaps between them. There are therapeutic solutions available to us, but we tend to take them only when the gap reaches a crescendo—perhaps it is too late by then. With the advent of COVID-19, these psycho-therapeutic gaps can come up between two closely related people, even friends. We need to be conscious of them and work on them. Only then will the sunshine and clouds meet at a certain plane.

GOOD OR BAD, BE READY

As we have transitioned from an operating business to a strategic one, and now into philanthropy and investment portfolios, as an entrepreneur, I have been keenly watching the changes happening in our business world. I have run Globsyn Group operationally for more than 22 years and have now handed it over to my sons, Rahul and Romit. As I look back at my corporate life, I realise that there is one particular area that has undergone massive structural, behavioural and institutional change, particularly in the knowledge and technology industry. And that area is the Human Resources (HR) department.

In our days, HR was a key area for organisational efficacy and growth. HR used to control aspects of human professional development and growth through various initiatives in the organisation, with full support from the management. We used to say that they—the HR—are also the eyes and ears of the people in the company. There was also an element of organisational control exercised through the HR by the management. The approach was highly behavioural, and the solutions were worked out via one-on-one/face-to-face direct interactions. Performance was a key parameter in the evaluation process, along with behavioural aspects.

But things have evolved over the years, especially in the knowledge and technology industry. As the industry became number-driven, we discovered a new add-on terminology in 'Recruiters' who were not HR. Their job was mainly to recruit in large numbers, as our software industry grew. So, the target-setting started from there, as they needed billing, which was per person per hour. So far so good. The HR continued to do some good development work, understanding the capabilities of people, their growth and developmental needs, and plugged in those gaps. Then, when these parameters became paramount, the recruiters' role became critical, but they were controlled through operations and no more by the HR. Hence, the organisational structure kept changing.

The person who was Head of Operations became key. Head of HR became a supporting function. The numbers started growing in the organisation, teams performed, and their performance at work, or in production, became key evaluation criteria. Did the organisation's character change when this happened? Most certainly, it did. The new generation manager or the young entrepreneur perhaps did not see the earlier structure of HR to understand the change and as the growth in numbers was huge, his focus was predominantly on recruitment, delivery and yield. Most of the behavioural aspects took a backseat, not everywhere though; but they did become only a motivating or feel-good exercise conducted by the HR department. Training programmes became as per need, mostly in product training, and perhaps the behavioural needs got ignored.

We have always felt that behavioural HR not only builds the company and helps it perform in a healthy way, but also obliquely builds the society and social framework around it.

Do Corporates Always Play a Major Role in Building the Society?

The ecosystem and the positive well-being of their employees reverberates in the society. This impact of lack of behavioural development is being witnessed and felt by the society today. This impairs human development and growth as well—and I believe, it has. The reflection of this could be felt in leadership styles, teamwork, passion to excel, and going the extra mile to perform within the organisation every day. We must try and build a society where transactional and behavioural work can co-exist in good measure.

Let us seriously reflect on this and think. Otherwise, going forward, once again the lubricant will dry, or the software will be missing, and it will become all hardware and once it breaks, it will turn fatal, for sure.

CAUTION AND INTELLIGENCE

Over the past ten years or so, three companies in the global tech world have dominated the IT industry. They are Microsoft, Google and Facebook. They have influenced the lives and minds of a complete generation like never before. As long as they did well, from their direct business issues and manifested their growth to direct business terms, it was OK. But they have done a lot more.

Today's youth have almost forgotten the concept of 'real-life experiences', or learning from books, or even communicating with their friends and families through writing, reading or talking. They get these information or do these things through Google/Facebook/Instagram and not through experiences.

These will have a very serious fallout on the world as a whole, and the youth in particular. Misuse of any information or skill or technology is a natural human phenomenon, but parents might try and instill 'experience' as a serious learning mechanism, apart from studies. Today, when a general knowledge question like 'Who is the President of Ghana?' is asked to our son/daughter, he/she will quickly 'Google' the name and get the correct answer. We tend to forget that in his learning process, they did not learn that in a normal way. We heave a sigh of relief, say that the society

is changing, and then keep quiet. Is that enough? Or should we teach our kids how to learn from nature and their surroundings, and through challenges and interactions? Many of us, when we were kids, used to see our dad/mom read a novel or a story book even before a baby learnt to talk. We learnt that reading books was a good habit and tried to inculcate that habit in our system. But does that happen now?

The use of technology can be beneficial to a child's development and growth, but not always. The choice regarding the kind of use is very important. Internet, in general, contains seemingly innocuous data, which opens our learning and understanding curve, but the use of that data and its interpretations should be discussed as part of parenting. Or should we leave the child to make this choice on their own?

I will share a quick story about what one of my sons went through while he was studying in USA. Once he had an eye problem—the nerve cells in the eye were impacted, but nothing was visible from the outside. He checked the internet and wrote about his problem; soon, he received letters, notes and expressions from patients around the world with the same problem, most of them were seeking medical help for the same. Whether they had the same problem or different, we did not know, but what we did know was that my son was hugely upset, traumatised and worried after reading those stories of people who were at different stages of their lives, and suffering from related issues. He kept speaking to me and when I asked about where he got his information, he mentioned the internet. I told him to pack his bags and take the earliest flight back home. He returned. We took him to a proper eye hospital with specialists and by God's grace he is completely fine now. This happened some 15 years back.

There are issues with the overuse and misuse of internet and social platforms to gather information. Parenting in today's world is tricky. We need to accept that responsibility and deal with the mix of experience and technology with a lot of caution and intelligence.

TRANSITIONING THE BUSINESS

A lot has happened in my life, most of them were not planned or thought of, but they did change the course of my life—either permanently or temporarily, by changing the way I looked at life. There is an interesting observation here. If you are able to do or achieve in your personal/professional life what you had wished for, you start developing a stupid feeling at times that it will never stop. You think that the pace, intensity, passion, desire, hunger, and the sense of social justice with which you were driving

yourself will continue the same way. But the truth, my friends, is not so. Something will happen that will re-determine the course of your life with all its associated elements; and it will make you stop, or take a detour, to the least.

I had seriously felt 'contented', perhaps for the first time in my life, after my memoir released on 3 February 2018 with so much pomp and show. The arrival of my friends from all over the world, to be with me, provided a deep sense of satisfaction for the journey I had undertaken. My sons, Romit and Rahul, introduced me to that great audience—it was an emotional moment and I was simply HAPPY. But destiny had different plans. I broke my femur bone in New Jersey on the day I was supposed to travel back to India on 31 October; the subsequent surgery next day and the rehab that followed was not only time-consuming, but also very painful. This pain and recovery allowed me to spend a lot of time with myself—be it on the hospital bed in USA, or thereafter in India after my return on 3 December.

One very significant decision that I took, professionally speaking, at this time was convincing myself to hand over the business to my sons—operationally, fully—so that they could be in control. My role in the business would depend on what they would want me to do, and not the other way round. For a first-generation startup entrepreneur, who is hugely ambitious and has been struggling for all these years, to not look at your bank balance before the salary day and decide not to be involved in any form of P&L was a major call for me. Rahul-Romit, on their part, saw this as a huge opportunity for them to grow and excel in life. And why not? All these years, they have been learning the tricks of the trade from their dad, both nationally and globally, and were totally ready. The transition got completed and the fact that I was focusing on my recovery by being on the bed really helped them. I had promised to my family over a dinner, and in the presence of everyone, that no matter what I did, from that day onwards, I won't be controlling the P&L of any of our Group businesses. People who are in business will understand the seriousness of this decision made by me that day. So, if at all I was passionate about philanthropy, it was because that was the only way I could express and continue my spirit of giving. A big, big relief for me and 2018/19 became that fateful year.

So, people within the organisation and outside saw that it was not BDG calling the shots, but Rahul-Romit. It took them three months to soak in everything, and also for me to practice what I had preached. For every first-generation entrepreneur, this is a major event; and interestingly it all happened, informally, internally and without the involvement of lawyers, accountants and the administration.

FROM JONATHAN TO CHANG

It's usual practice that we get used to the life we always live and adjust to the life we aspire to have in future. Both happen to us often. It is just that what you aspire, your source is checked once in a while. As long as your source or intention is clear, you will meet your aspirations. But in the process, you are made to go through a journey wherein you know what your aspirations are, but have little knowledge about what all you have to face on your way. And if you do overcome the challenges with a smile, then your next goal comes easily to the forefront and gets clearer. Now coming to aspirations. What is their source? Many. But in my case it was a combination of several things—one's upbringing, one's immediate social environment, the ability to keep pushing oneself, the hunger or desire to excel, learn more and make a difference (these are also at times directly related to one's upbringing), and, maybe, a bit of external glamour like fame, glory, pride etc.

One more factor, perhaps, plays a major role in aspiration. It did for me, at least. And this is your innate purity. Your innocence and naivety. If you mix these with the above, your search factor in getting more out of your life turns into a balanced mix.

This, so far, is the Jonathan story.

Now, coming to my personal inspiration in life. I have not met Richard Bach, the author of *Jonathan Livingstone Seagull*, but he doesn't know what he has done to me, and many entrepreneurs like me, who grew up reading his book and got inspired. I have shared the book with many friends, Globsyn youngsters and students.

Now, come to another character he created in the same book, which is where I am headed to. This character is called Chang. When Jonathan started feeling like he had achieved virtually everything that he ever wanted to, and started flying higher and higher, he met Chang, at a place where Jonathan believed no one could have ever gone.

He asked him: 'What are you doing here?'

Chang said: 'I live here. For many years.'

Chang has a different life and story from that of Jonathan. So, what is Chang's story? Having achieved all that Jonathan had achieved, and living in this space alone for so many years, what does Chang do?

MAKE FRIENDS, TOUCH UPON DIVERSITY

We had a very special annual reunion of select members of our HBS OPM38 Adventure Group. We were to complete our first leg of commitment, of meeting every year in a new continent for the next six years, and this was the sixth year. Africa, Asia, Australia, Europe, South America and North America were the continents, and Tanzania, India, Adelaide, Norway, Mexico and USA were the regions, that we covered as part of our commitment.

Congrats to all! Over a span of six years, we have grown very close to one another, professionally, personally and family-wise. We have also travelled the world together, seen and discovered things together, shared our rich heritage and culture together—why we do and why we

don't do certain things—and at this stage of our life, it has been wonderful, to say the least.

Just imagine, until May 2007 I didn't even know that I would meet such wonderful people from different corners of the globe. And today, we are best of friends. Such is life. Let us hope that this kind of friendship, with mutual respect, love, care and fun, will last forever. To some of them, with whom I have grown closer over the years, I say, 'Thank you so much for your care, generosity and wisdom.' I wish to carry these through to the next part of my life.

MANAGING PEOPLE – NO STRAIGHT JACKET FORMULA

There is always this thought that we need to tell our people what to do. Then there is this thought, that if you give them freedom, and not micro-manage, they perform better. Over time, I have experienced that neither is absolutely true. It is a queer mix, which evolves from your style of working over the years, your own learning curve, your ways of handling people, and your ability to think beyond yourself, which creates a chemistry you and your team are most comfortable with. You tend to follow that.

Another key factor to the governance issue in corporate working is for others to see, know and understand (from you) why you do what you do. As more and more of that becomes clear to them, the chemistry of working parameters evens out. If you are doing something for a cause, there will be some who will always be with you, as they support that cause themselves. Others will be with you, if you are helping them grow their careers by providing good and exciting work opportunities; there will also be some, who will simply work with you, as they keep learning from the environment you create for work.

But if you do not have these, or any other reason, they keep seeking these either from you, or from their immediate supervisors, or from the company in general. Once they do not find any of these, they might look for better compensation packages, which may act as the sole motivator to be around. Pressure at times is killing. Once pressurized they tend to succumb. Some again, excel under pressure. So, it is interesting. You cannot put any of these into a straight-jacket mode. It is a human being you are dealing with. So, the procedure is not robotic. It changes and behaves differently all the time.

You got to be there in it, to feel, understand and evolve a mechanism that is most convenient to you. Give it time. Be clear about yourself. Whatever you are doing, know why you are doing it. You will see things opening up automatically for you.

NEW MANAGER IS CONFUSED!

The business world has really changed a lot in the past 25 years or so. Today, to run a niche, high on value, mid-sized company where individuals are respected and rewarded for their deeds also needs to take a lot on themselves. Therefore, it is becoming pretty difficult to run or manage a company like this.

When you run such a company, the very nature of governance of such an enterprise evolves, which is definitely not the case with a well-oiled, structured organisation.

So, when this niche company starts growing, experts tend to tell you (all the time): 'Listen mate, you need to have a clear plan, budget, roles and targets and job descriptions.' When you do that, they will then perhaps tell you, 'See, I told you. You are falling short in 7 areas to achieve this goal, so they are non-starters.' But I keep pleading to them that they let us not firm everything. Let us develop this business model, and then let us see the loose ends; and we will keep working on them and remove the blocks, and grow. I also tell them I have a young bunch of managers who are good in this method of working.

That is not always understood or appreciated. Is that the time for the entrepreneur to go? Not really. Because the 'evolving' model of business is also a proven model of business, and it works. So, you need to create a blend. This is where the current generation of managers, who are driven by huge peer pressure and are acting like MNCs (with the advent of MNCs and 'Big' Indian companies) need to introspect a little. These managers who keep quizzing this niche company's manager about 'Why are you doing all this?' 'Are you getting your value for money?' need to understand this—such questions tend to confuse a manager who has been learning till date in this niche company. They (managers of the niche company) then start thinking, 'Why am I doing this really?'

So, a prospective 'Learning Manager' fails or falls into this deadly trap. As India marches into this new world of growth, there will be an emergence of many of these 'niche' companies that actually produce talent, cleans them up, and creates huge potential for delivery in this society. Young, budding managers must have a close look at themselves, and ask whether they want to be the new generation 'Learning Managers', or succumb to the load of implementing everything.

MY REAL TARGET: THE YOUTH

When I went to Harvard at this ripe age in 2007, there was something that was bothering me. It was the ability to govern a complex organisation that was growing. There were so many gaps that needed to be bridged. It was my wife who reminded me of the need to address these gaps. She said, 'Whom do you learn from every day? Everyone seems to be looking up to you to learn.' That's when I decided that I must embrace further learning, and went to Harvard Business School. I sat in a classroom for three years, going back every year, till my graduation was completed from such a prestigious institution. Learning is a personal thing. Statistics say, adults don't learn, unless they want to. They cannot be taught.

Over the past four years, and after my surgical fixing in Cleveland Clinic, I have realised that I have transformed. But one thing keeps driving me, and it is the relentless pursuit of opportunities. I don't know why, but I get excited whenever an opportunity hits me. My wife keeps complaining: 'Why do you need to do more? There is so much on your plate today. Why don't you do what you are doing today, better?'

But I never think that way. Not doing my job well has never occurred to me. I also do not pursue opportunities because of that. I pursue the unknown and what excites me is the risk, the newness, the adventure; and making a business successful by taking advantage of all the available opportunities is my benchmark. I have recently structured my businesses. I now have my sons getting into it, bringing in fresh thinking and fresh areas of work. So, now we are into retail, food, healthcare, etc. There is a sense of fulfilment when I look back at what I have been able to do for the people so far—from the time they studied Engineering and went to my Software Finishing

School, then worked in Infinity/Crystals, my intelligent building complexes, developed Software (Globsyn Infotech) and looked at Management education (Business School) and then benefited from skill development (Globsyn Skills), especially the non-computer science guys and different industry segments to now, when their personal needs in retail, food and healthcare (Globsyn Innoventure) are being looked at.

Am I doing too many things? I don't think so. I am still serving the same clients since 1996—the youth. I will continue to do that, as my core businesses also keep growing. It's interesting, isn't it? That is what keeps me going. When my son Romit asked me what should be the vision statement of the new company INNOVENTURES that he is driving, I said, 'Developing new ideas about new ideas.'

RELENTLESS PURSUIT OF OPPORTUNITIES: SKILLS

Many of us do business with internal contradictions, which is one of the reasons why many of us do not build a large organisation, unlike say Reliance or Infosys. Different approaches, but both hugely successful. One may work on clearing the blocks to grow, while the other may take some quick right decisions to grow laterally, through IPOs, ADR, GDRs, etc. and then use that money wisely, with astute man management.

For many of us, pursuing our passion takes a lot out of us and at times, it becomes overwhelming to grow laterally. As a result, it could feel like we are playing a snake and ladder game all the time, but we are on course for pursuing our passion of what we wanted to do. Doing that individually is different from doing it institutionally.

One such opportunity came on a platter to me in October 2011, when through a contact I met officials of NSDC (National Skill

Development Corporation) who were pursuing the huge dream of making India skilled. This has been a major influence in my own life, and my own growth; and over the years, I have seen how a youngster benefits through structured skilled training and becomes a performing individual in the corporate world. I was very driven by this. Till then, I had focused on skills related to technology and management, which to me had always seemed like two sides of the same coin. Now, I saw an opportunity to pursue my passion of contributing to the grand project of making a 'Skilled India' by taking up this exercise, with skilling for employability as my credo.

Over the past 15 years, we have taken students from Tier-2 or Tier-3 engineering colleges, and through our propriety software framework product Knowledge Finishing School (KFS), we have transformed them into strong entry-level engineers for the software industry. I have seen the difference we have been able to bring in the lives of over 75,000 youngsters. A happy smile on the faces of these students, and their parents, has also been very satisfying. Now, I was dreaming of doing the same for 1 million people, in 10 years, from 21 industry segments; if we have enough will to make this happen, what a mind-boggling experience it will be!

So, Globsyn Skills got formed with NSDC as our JV (Joint Venture) partner, with equity and seat in the board. We went on to start hiring and put the plan in place. It was sheer excitement for all of us at Globsyn. We have another 20 years of work to do now. We have, perhaps, finally given shape to the first 'not ONLY for profit' enterprise.

EDUCATION-SKILLS-TECHNOLOGY

We have come a long way in Globsyn. Our first offering in 1996 was YSM. The Software Finishing School concept was brought into the business horizon by us. During those days many did not really understand what we were trying to do. I was totally clear. My mentor, Prof Biswajit Nag, told me, 'You have picked up an area, which will keep you perpetually in business.' 'Keep filling the gaps in the education system, always.'

That's what we have done by and large. Our technology background has helped us make use of technology liberally to make our delivery efficient, and increase our reach to consumers. It has helped our students learn better, and in an organized way. Using technology, we have delivered education, training and skill development to our consumers. To facilitate this, we have built infrastructure, used that to hedge our fund requirements, built campuses, kept the engine running for our software services business and in the midst of all this, we acquired a software company that was listed, and then sold off the listing after five years, while keeping the main business of payment solutions in our Mumbai office.

Then NSDC happened. After three years of agony, we suddenly had the STAR scheme. That changed the course. We had for years not seen volumes in any of our businesses. This time, it was real. The 400+ centres across India delivered over 30,000 qualified students, and we topped banking and finance nationally—a great achievement for a fledgling outfit.

Rahul led it admirably well. It was mainly his doing. Passionate, straightforward, committed and high on energy, Rahul reminded me of my young days in PCL.

ARE YOU THE PROBLEM CHILD?

After you have had a very successful professional life, especially in the eyes of others, that came with a huge fan-following, and not having to report to anyone for the past 30+ years or so, and the freedom to run your own company, there comes a time when one has to pass on the baton to someone else, a professional, your son, or someone suited to do the job; and this becomes an issue for many reasons. If you are the person concerned, then you start thinking, planning, and developing work patterns to enable the transition and since you are mentally ready to do that, it happens smoothly in say six months, or in a year or two, if it's your family business.

In this, what many do not factor in is that while you are doing this, you are also passing on authority, power, control of people and systems to someone or some team, without the prospect of replacement, or getting back; you are left with none of it, quite quickly, and the high-profile fast-paced job/work, which you pursued so passionately for so many years, is GONE! This void creates multiple issues on many fronts. First, you are only used to people listening to you, and don't have the habit to listen to anyone else. You always had a team of people at your beck and call to do most of your work, as you decided over the proceedings; you are too used to being fed with data only, for you to take all the decisions.

Now, you are given decisions and you need to agree upon. This is new to you. If it's a family business and the relationship is between the father and the son/s, it also has emotions added in the process. The sons grow faster, as they are exposed to the world much earlier than you, even as everything done by you was meant to prepare them to be the decision-makers of tomorrow; and they start deciding over you, as you are the first target. So, if the company is not structured well and decision-making styles are changing down the generations, thereby, giving way to multipoint decisions instead of single-point decision-making, there is bound to be communication gaps.

This, quite frankly, is one of the most difficult phases of life, as the person who is the creator of the group of business ends up becoming the 'problem child' in decision-making, thereby, redundant and irrelevant. Funny, but true. Many of us have dealt with this situation. Our acumen, wisdom, tenacity and maturity will be under severe scrutiny in this transition process, especially if it's a new business that you have got into while you are in transition. This note of mine might help some people who are or will go through these situations; it will help them prepare themselves and deal with the transition better, with a much larger sense of understanding than others.

Life can be complex, even if you are simple.

SECTION TWO

JOURNEY TO HEALING

Take a deep breath, let's heal from within.
Join me on a journey of self-discovery

GIVE UP YOUR FEAR, TAKE THE NEXT STEP

As you keep repeating certain segments of your life over a period of time, you must tell yourself that it is time to move on. The hugely active segment of one's life is our middle life. There is a tendency to carry on with it as it has all the social domains around us, because it helps us to compare, and feel acceptable and acknowledged by what is called a society, which gives a sense of recognition and legitimacy to many.

Hence, we keep doing the same things over and over, and our journey turns repetitive. I call it the 'Segment 2' of our lives. But if you care to look back at your inquisitive self, childhood expectations and learning curve, you may find that it is time to travel further. The devil resides in us; it holds us back and more often than not, we fall prey to it. Society keeps talking about mediocrity, repetitiveness, social obligations, commitments in a hugely glorified way, with only one objective—to keep us tied down to routine, with little or no self-development. We are happy in a world where we have the 'Power' to control and less questions are asked.

But where is the freedom to move on? For hundreds of years, humans have been kept under a leash, without realising that they have been controlled by a thought or power that wants to control them, while making them feel that everything happens around them. Funny, isn't it?

For one would then never learn the fun of growth, unless one dares to take the NEXT STEP towards freedom. When you do that, everything around you starts to look and feel different. All the people around you in 'Segment 2' look mundane to the same 'You'; a lot of space gets created for you to absorb new things, look at them in a new way, and show you the path to make a significant impact on people and yourself, and above all you feel FREE. You are with people who have travelled with you, maybe earlier, and then together you begin a new journey, a new destination, a new way to eradicate miseries of people and create a new leadership dimension. Life suddenly becomes worth living and then you wonder: 'Why didn't I do this earlier?'

This concept of taking people to the next level is a continuous process. WE ALL GROW DIFFERENTLY. So, there comes a time, depending on the decisions you take in life, when you discover yourself in a very different way. There is of course a huge set of intelligent, extremely well-read and educated people who understand this, but defend their decision to remain in the well by holding on to things like culture, value, social embargo and education, to find answers for their actions/inactions or decisions/lack of decisions. Since when did not doing and status quo become a wise thing? You do meet gurus in your life who change your complete perspective, the way of looking at life, with some convincing stories. They bring that dynamism that you see in a flowing river. Imagine a river with a dam on it, it forgets to flow over the boulders on its own sweet will. Instead, it gets sluggish.

The Buddha taught us how to look at life. But trust me, even societies and cultures change, or move, albeit very slowly, but like the politicians, it is always advisable for the mind to keep the intelligent people under control through fear and religion, invoking the self-created concept of right and wrong, and continue happily. Mostly the so-called 'mind rulers' win, if you see it over a small period of time.

But people like us, who have ventured to discover ourselves, experimented with experiences thrown at us in life, used and absorbed them and created new dimensions of life and growth, have this hope that one day, people whom we wanted to be with us, will come—maybe they are on the way, maybe they will realise what the hell they are doing by leading a stereotypical, controlled life of right and wrong, even as god has given them so much of intellectual understanding. They will surely come on board soon.

We badly want them here. We always wanted them. We are missing them hugely today. We are told today that this will also pass, and you will grow over it. But I ask, 'Why?' We did not want it to pass. We did not want to grow past them. We wanted to grow with them—together and on a very different scale and dimension than today.

MY JOURNEY TO THE INFINITE

My journey of life has always opened up new dimensions, teaching me to accept, learn and grow. It is simply fascinating. Many times, we are so engrossed in our own fixed thinking of right and wrong that we even doubt our own growth potential. For me, however, that has never happened. Fortunately, I started growing and loved experimenting, evolving, facing newer challenges, and taking risks—all of which are needed for growth and self-development. I never needed to plan my journey. I rather learnt from it. All I did was to keep squeezing my intelligence and my energies to deliver more.

But over last 8-10 years, I took a conscious decision to stop, and then I set my new trajectory. I have always been a very keen learner. I am very inquisitive about new things, so my process of self-development and self-actualization led me on the path of huge learning. It was a journey that initially even I was not prepared to tread. I took time to

understand, but then it became clear. This is also a time when I took trips to Bhutan. These were not simple tours, rather they were a part of my spiritual journey, from finite to infinite. The soft floating clouds across the towering mountain scape taught me lessons that even my decades of excellently structured job life could not teach.

I was completely lost in absorbing a new dimension of 'spirituality' and the finite part of my journey gave way to infinite learning. I discovered a new state of matter, beyond the scope of solid, liquid and gas, as written in Physics books. And that feeling started to take shape as I internalised it. But I was alone. Since I still had to complete a few tasks in the finite world—I needed to connect with that world too, and then the transition would be complete. I needed help. Everyone does. As I was amidst the clouds during my Bhutan trips, the mountains impacted me spiritually. But I also needed to relate, share with other souls as none understood my feelings. As luck would have it, I found souls who could relate, but they too could not leave their finite space. They loved living in their finite world of luxury and only lectured on spiritual journey, refusing to take the actual plunge in the search of infinity. I was prepared though.

But they were caught in the whirlpool of material world, they were not free. They were tied to so many inhibitions of fear, loss and insecurities. They could not come with me. Maybe, someday, they will. I, thus, questioned myself as to why people who travel intellectually understand the value of spiritual integration with our finite world, but still cling to the social fabric that gives them comfort? Do they fear the unknown? They even doubt people like us who are ready to partake that spiritual path and doubt our intentions, as that helps them justify their own selfish intentions to hold back. But for how long? The pull of the infinite is so strong, that, trust me, very soon all the shackles will break loose and make them free too.

Believe me, that day is not far. We will again join hands and be together. I am already on that path. Just tread on it, else you will never know what you did not experience!

IS SURGERY ONLY A PHYSICAL EXERCISE?

My molar teeth, four of them, have been giving me problems for a while. The toothache at times is unbearable. I remember when I went to Boston last year to attend the HBS reunion, I could not go to the most important meeting; I stayed back at the Four Seasons Hotel, as I was writhing in pain. So, suddenly when my dentist said that I would have to extract them, I felt like why not? I have always been naive in life. It has also been my strength, in its own way. I did not realise what this extraction

meant, especially when it involved extracting all of my four molars at one go. It meant hospitalisation and general anaesthesia. And the minute my ignorance about the procedure was taken over by facts, that's when my problem started.

Three days after the extraction when I was released from the hospital, I was detected with a prostrate issue. So, I went from Belle Vue to Medica Hospital, where my urologist/nephrologist admitted me. Medica's warm hospitality made me feel good and on 4 May 2016, I had a second surgery under general anaesthesia. All went well, and I was released on 9 May and returned home. For the next two weeks, I was at home, recovering, taking life easy and 'thinking'. That's what I do when I get time, to keep my little grey cells active and running.

From 25 April through 9 May, it was hospital time for me. For me, these are periods in my life that have always been very productive, as I unconsciously keep searching for connects to progress in life. When you do that, unknowingly, the connect happens and such connects rejuvenate me and all my verve comes back.

TO LIVE OR NOT TO LIVE!

When I returned from USA, my life was so hectic that I travelled in and out every second night, with luggage, into airports and out. This was kind of taking a toll on me, but I was with family and friends, so there was no pressure and I felt I can somewhat stretch myself. On my return again, I quickly decided to go to Bangalore for a day—my reason for doing this, many would feel, defied logic, but I still did it. On my return, I had this major presentation to be made to my new MBA students starting their session in Globsyn. The talk lasted for two hours.

On my way back, I could feel a chill, a fever that was invading my body. I could feel the sickness, tiredness and such symptoms that overshadows your energy level. On return, I slept, but by the time I reached home, my fever had skyrocketed. I was literally shivering, and suddenly I felt out of control. That was 28 July 2015. After several medicines, doctors, I still felt very weak. No fever, but the aftermath of what is called a viral still loomed large. On the second night, my wife felt that I would have to be shifted to the hospital, as I was not in my senses; I was shivering and was not in control. But somehow, I withstood that. My doctor was calm and instructed my wife as to what should be done. The same day, in the morning, I remember, I was not able to get up on my own. I thought it was a 'joke' and

started smiling. My wife also did not believe. But the truth was that I was not able to get up. I tried and tried and tried. Finally, my wife put in a lot of effort to pull me up. Wow!

I never ever felt like that before. The viral had sapped all my energy. Despite its cruel head popping up to squeeze my body, this episode of viral fever was a big 'healing experience' for me; it was a time when I travelled within. I realised so many things at one go. 'Yes, yes, yes. I will listen to my inner soul from now on. I will try and match my mind and body to some degree, so that there is a balance between these two. Only then, I can lead a decent life,' I told myself.

I know, it might sound 'boring' to me, or someone like me, who has always been driven by passion, high energy, and a drive of the mind, without caring for the body so much. This may seem like a kind of let down to such people.

THE JOY OF 'ALONE-NESS'

When I was at the IIT KGP hostel during my student days, it was always difficult for me to be alone. I always had friends around me. Even during study time, I would go to someone's room and study. I really didn't know why. No, I was not scared of anything but yes, there was a certain element of comfort when I had others around me.

Over the years, this continued. I was always a people's person. Talking, conducting meetings, giving presentations, convincing people to think the way I do—these have been a part and parcel of a major portion of my professional life. I loved travelling all over the world, meeting the best of minds in business and other well-known dignitaries, and sharing my thoughts with them, but more importantly I learnt a lot from most of them. There were years in my professional life wherein I would have travelled for over 250 days in a year to different countries, in different time zones, mostly all by myself. I used to say jocularly that I visited Madame Tussauds on my fourteenth visit to London. I had not found the time to do this earlier. That was my life. This lasted for about eight years. God has been really kind to me for giving me this exposure.

Then came a point of time in my life when I started growing and evolving as a person, horizontally, after growing vertically. Vertical growth had given me huge professional landmarks and achievements, but horizontal growth led me to the path of self-discovery. Then I began the process of self-actualization. Once you start doing that, and it happened to me naturally (as most of the things had happened earlier), I just wanted to be with myself. That's when I realised and absorbed the actualization process. The 'high' of being 'alone' but never 'lonely' dawned on me. Questions about understanding

the 'self' and who I am became a dominant part of my journey. It attracted me hugely. This was the time when I frequently travelled to Bhutan and fell in love with that place, enjoying my solitude. The same guy who used to go to his friend's room to study, travelled without work for 8-10 days to Bhutan, all by himself, and was mentally occupied completely. I saw things in life from a different perspective, which was something that I had never seen before. A complete transformation, thus, happened.

Watching the thin clouds floating, crossing the huge mountains fearlessly and traversing their path, was an endearing sight for me every morning at Thimpu, the capital of Bhutan. So, was my 54th-floor apartment's terrace in Dubai, from where I could watch both tall buildings and a large number of tiny-looking cars on the roads, as well as the expanse of the vast sky, the half-moon, admiring my 'alone-ness'. It feels lovely and revives all my energies, and with renewed vigour, I deep dive into strategic thoughts and the intellectual journeys of life, which I have lived and, god willing, would live a bit more.

LIFE IS A CONTINUUM

When you seem to have achieved a lot in the eyes of your well-wishers, and successfully transitioned your business to your next generation happily and things keep moving on, then, how do you look ahead in life? How do you engage yourself meaningfully and continue to do things that continue to engage you? How do you keep creating and developing? The motivation might at times be low and you start using words like 'retirement' and get some kind of social acceptance for yourself. So, what do you do?

First of all, we must believe that LIFE is a continuum. It's not a start to end journey. Though, for this generation there is still a few more years, in this world, but once you move past that period, you would be gone, turning into dust. But it's very important to understand that the journey is continuing to develop, grow and add, even as it becomes more matured, with the ever-changing roles. Though the body becomes physically weak, our soul keeps moving with the same intensity. The easiest way to address this is to keep doing what you were doing, and creating, in a more intense and deep way, so that your relevance of doing that work keeps enhancing.

If it is difficult to understand, let me try and explain with my own creations. Recently we did an excellent, new kind of Broadway programme called *Ma Ashbei* at the Calcutta Broadway. After the humungous effort, we needed to plan the direction in which we wanted to move ahead. While we do have my Dad's (Late Sukamal Dasgupta) *Baneer Beena*, which is now available in all music channels and will be promoted to reach more people, especially those who love songs and compositions by Rabindranath Tagore, Atul Prasad and Nazrul Islam, or similar lyrics-dominated music/songs. When I looked ahead, to recharge my creative energies further, I thought of opening a music and dance learning channel, especially for the not-so-privileged youngsters who cannot afford to go to a renowned learning academy.

Our channel will offer them a similar quality of learning by opening two windows, one for music and the other for dance, on the CB (Calcutta Broadway) website. The website is meant for talented youngsters who come from challenging backgrounds. Such youngsters can come and learn the same for free, or at a negligible cost. Through this, talent can be promoted and given access to learning music and dance. Now to turn this idea to reality, I am aware that technology will play an important role in this project—technology would need to be licensed and developed so that the student can simply walk in and learn the way he/she would like to learn in a physical environment. That is what needs to be built first. So, I have now set my mind on getting this activated... This is what I call a continuum.

THE 4TH QUADRANT

Every intelligent human being passes through various learning curves as they grow in life; and as they do so, they add to themselves, altering their current state of intelligence, thoughts and feelings. For example, an intelligent person at the age of 15 will add different things to his/her current status than the same person at the age of 21, 29, 36, 42 and so on. While this journey continues, their exposure, experiences and intellect keep maturing over the years, thereby, forming a structure within their brain. We call this their current vision, thoughts, imagination or intellect. At all these stages of life, they keep modifying their thoughts through their experiences, learning, situations and understanding—all of which makes them wiser.

But people are of different kinds. There are some who, in their own eyes, stop growing once they have achieved what they wanted to. Logical but limited. Again, there are a few, like me, who, having reached a particular level in our learning curve, feel that they should try and go back to zero and start learning yet again, by taking it in their stride, guided by whatever they have learnt so far. It's like the Pandavas' journey to heaven. Some fell along the way, and only one succeeded to reach the top. Personally, for me, when I am in a sombre mood and think of my own journey in life, I am very surprised, to say the least. For the first few years, intellectually my growth was manageable and could be comprehended. But in the past 12-15 years, the intellectual growth multiplied manifold, far beyond my own comprehension. At times, there were several dots in the growth curve, but the summation was perfect and satisfying.

What does that mean? It means that there have been situations, which I have lived through without completely understanding why

I did what I did, and then looked back, only to see that what I did was indeed heartening. It's a crazy path. So, I decided not to think about it too much and break my perceived journey into small blocks for the future, even if there were dots, as I could not plot everything in those blocks. So, my life now has become a journey of dots, lines and graphs and as they emerge within me, some of the dots get connected. The only problem I face when that happens is that many of my friends, associates, not to speak of my family, misunderstand me. But I tell myself that that's a cost I will have to pay to keep learning and experiencing life in its true colours, as all the things that happen are not always understood. But the common key is to keep yourself open-minded. I tend to share the same example—about the 4th quadrant of the rectangle being open—with many of you. The idea is simple: in an otherwise closed life, how fresh thoughts and ideas flow in through that open 4th quadrant and make life more meaningful. And for me, this is what completes my journey.

CONTRADICTIONS OF AN ADULT MIND

As a student of Behaviourial Science and its natural development with age and time, I have noticed different people respond to different situations differently. At times, they do realise through their intelligence and wisdom that their acts make no sense, but the society has kept them shackled for so many years that to break free from those shackles is a big task. Luckily for me, I have had phenomenal freedom of mind and expression, and have continued to remain free from any such bondages like parental, cultural and social norms. We are being constantly told with a dash of fright that if we break the barriers put in by the society at large, we shall land in trouble.

Here I am, referring to traditional values combined with knowledge, education, intelligence, wisdom and the spirit of freedom, experimentation, discovery and internal growth. Several barriers come up while we are tempted to pursue growth. So, we withdraw mostly and assume that we shall not suffer from guilt. As intellectual freedom and growth of the mind are intangible and very personal, it is simple to cover it up by not pursuing and freeing yourself from the apparent guilt syndrome. What you lose is often not quantifiable and highly intellectual as a

stimulus, partly cultural as well. So, it is not difficult to suppress.

The question I am asking today is why do we do this? Our education encourages and disappoints us. Intangibles force us to change and stop us from changing too much, or beyond a particular stage. Why do these contradictory things happen?

It is most certainly depriving the society of its intellectual growth, but you can also turn around and say, 'I don't want that kind of growth, which can make my life difficult, make me feel guilty and apparently I can do without it.'

True. But I am still referring to the intellectual loss we go through because of this. Perhaps a day and time will come in this society, when such thoughts on intellectual progression will become the most sought-after research element in higher education (to begin with), and then later on become the norm. People like us won't be there then, but the spark of ignition that we generated will have more takers, if we can convert our idealistic thoughts to real-life data, which will help researchers look into this subject seriously and initiate deeper discussions.

FROM BDG TO BIKRAM

As I sit in my suite in Le Meridien, Thimpu, Bhutan, looking at the clouds and mountains playing outside, I start my process of decoding BDG. I don't even remember when it all happened, or how it happened. My huge energy to make a difference in whatever I do, a trifle better, became systemic within me. I started doing this in everything I did, in life, work, home, social relations, and it became 'Me'. It is somewhere here, I think, work results started showing and in the eyes of everyone else and those who were around, they felt that energy in me, and started responding in any way they could. This is how I started being referred to as BDG. And today, when I start thinking about it, I shudder to think whether

I can get the Bikram back in me. It's been many years of professional experiences, achievements, failures, reactions, responses, anger, not wanting to lose ever, but looking at his people with compassion, at the end of a hard day's work, taking personal interest in them, caring for them, and sharing his experiences and values with them, while admonishing them for mistakes, and being disappointed with failures, perhaps partially summarizes BDG over the past 29 years. Maybe it does. Maybe, it doesn't. Others are better judges of him.

Who was Bikram? Very few people know him. If I say, he was an innocent, naive, shy and a highly positive person, but with little exposure, who wanted to enjoy his life, do theatre, recite and organize events and functions, take/carry people along, will you believe that? Maybe not. Bikram enjoyed the hills, loved to travel and be with people. He failed miserably, when others had different ideas and motives, as he thought. He didn't know, whether he will express himself, or withdraw. It was always a Hobson's choice for him. But he was surely fun-loving.

This Bikram became BDG.

Now he wants to get back to his 'Bikramhood'. 'Is it possible?' he keeps asking. One option is that if he gets out of the life of all the people who call him BDG, and develops his life around people who call him Bikram (Da), and then be with more and more of such people, as he goes along. So, BDG reduces, and Bikram increases. Possible? Practical? Is that what he wants? Let's see.

BHUTAN: MY JOURNEY OF SELF-DEVELOPMENT

I have been planning to go to Bhutan all by myself for a while. This urge to go, all by myself, has nothing to do with anyone, including my family. My family is everything to me. But over these past few years, I have developed this liking for solitude. I have really started enjoying being alone. I do not feel 'lonely' when I am 'alone'. On the contrary, I feel fully rejuvenated, happy, peaceful, and full of verve. So, when I started to go to Singapore, all by myself, every month from 15 January onwards, it was the beginning. But in Singapore, I realised that there was this faint pull to bring me back to the mundane life I have led for the last 30-odd years. I did not find that exciting. So, I went to places such as the Buddha Tooth Relic Temple and Museum, and the Haw Par Villa (Tiger Balm Garden). The scorching rays of the sun, notwithstanding, I tried to create that space for myself. But I was not really getting there, I felt. I did not know what? I did not know why? But I still felt as I have always felt

in my life, and kept saying: 'There is more to life.'

So, when my wife, Ranjana (Babli) went to Mayawati, with her aunts and cousin, a long-time desire of hers, I thought this could be my opportunity as well. So, on 4 June 2015, I left for Bhutan. It was absolutely open-ended, and I was happy and full of energy. I was looking into the unknown with a lot of hope, to discover myself.

My four days in Bhutan did exactly that to me. I was engaged with myself. Looking at the hills, driving through the hills and Dochula Pass, sitting by the river banks, watching the 169 feet high Buddha statue, spending time at the health club and the swimming pool, having a late breakfast, and an even late lunch, having soup only for dinner, going for morning walks near the golf course and finally the three-hour sessions with my monk (guruji) Myank R. Tulku, going through different aspects of Buddhism, relating them with myself, sharing my views on them, and understanding why and how these philosophies have become so powerful and what drives them. It was a fantastic trip that helped me look into the depths of my soul.

I came back full of it, and even today, I am full of it. I have been able to look internally within myself. I can see where I am. I can find peace with myself and my journey in life. So, I want to continue doing it as long as I can keep finding joy in it.

A SEAGULL'S LIFE: FLY, FLY, FLY...

Any settled life is a sign of stagnation, of mediocracy and boredom. We tend to do the same things again and again and again. For me, when I came to Dubai, I did not know for how long I would be here. After four months, the question of Visa started to come up—what kind of visa, the duration of my stay, NRI status, etc. Meanwhile, a restless guy like me completed a serious investment in a luxury restaurant, encompassing an area of 22,000 square feet, with three floors that had a fine dining area, a lounge bar and a rooftop evening club. It was a new business completely dominated by our partner Chef Mohammed, who had started this restaurant with a few investors, and we became the last one (investor) and took a majority stake in it.

Now what? I started planning for the future. I knew I would go back to India and then come back to Dubai again. It was tough to conceive living in Kolkata for six months with elections, heat, and

rains around the corner. So, I came up with the idea of Bhutan. I thought that maybe if I go to Bhutan, in the peak of summer to cool myself off, it will be a good break. So, Bhutan started getting added. Then we said, if we are doing that, why not open a subsidiary of our tech business in Bhutan and also have a training centre. Thus, a new business is born in a new location. This is how we are. This is what we keep doing. If the idea is new, as of today, we will work on it from tomorrow and hopefully come out with something interesting. So, if we look at life in Dubai, Bhutan, India, divided almost equally for the year, do we have enough floating variety? Enough weather baiters? If not, we need to create variety within the system again. This is the seagull's life. Flying from one shore to the other, searching, discovering, developing and growing. What a great life!

CAN I CHANGE THE COURSE OF MY LIFE?

I have travelled through my life, with a lot of verve, energy, passion and at times worked at break-neck speed. This is with reference to how others saw it. In my case, I was trying to do 'something' all these years. I have started asking this question now to myself: what was I seeking? All of us are victims of our own upbringing. Our insecurities get transplanted inadvertently through our parents into us and we start living that life, a life that is not completely our own.

So, we do not lead our life, but the one that is transplanted. Education gives us the courage to think independently. The same well-meaning parents, who have passed on their insecurities on to us, put us in a good school and college so that we do well in life. A good school helps us build our confidence a lot. You are surrounded by confident boys and girls, confident teachers and there is a huge learning. This is a second transplantation, which happens. If you miss out on a good school, your insecurities stay in your system. You would have to deal with it later in life.

In my case, I was lucky to start performing in my work life very early. I got many breaks, and I started taking more risks. I was enjoying the unpredictable. I could allow

my mind to fly, as the environment in HCL allowed me to do so, and I grew instantly. But then, so did my risk-taking instinct and expectations.

When I got on my own completely, I was by then trying to deal with the myth that surrounded me. So, on the one hand I had the passion and creative instincts to pursue my convictions, and on the other, I had to respond to the enormous challenges that I had imbibed from my value system to deliver and live as per set norms. There were huge contradictions in them. But I was driven to perform. So, perhaps I did what was almost impossible to do. I took in the contradictions through my mind and body and the physiological system had to deal with it. Society continued to see me perform, I continued to be revered and valued because of the fresh ideas and creative dimensions I brought in.

But in the middle of all this came the news of the impending damage I had caused to my body and the metabolic system. The contradictions took a toll on me and I needed to fix my system

clinically, to be ready to fight again. It did bring in a very vital question in my mind. Why am I doing what I am doing? Why do I have to respond to the expectations all the time? Whom am I doing this for? Haven't I already given to the society enough to digest, absorb and assimilate?

So, now, with the so-called success in the corporate world that I have undoubtedly achieved, my inner self questions me continuously, that is it time for me, to let go and bask in the glory of fresh rains, floating clouds and soothing music, and live in that serene calmness for the rest of my life? Can I do that?

CLEVELAND CLINIC AND LIFE'S LESSONS

I would be failing, if I did not write about this beautiful place where I spent the past 55 days. Cleveland was my home for almost two months. I came here with a specific mission to really know how I can address some of my health issues. But landed up doing much more and left the place completely rejuvenated, young and happy, raring to go, and completely fresh; in my over 30 years of work life, I have had the most relaxed time here.

If Harvard is the signature place for Business School, Cleveland, most certainly, is for cardiac ailments. Harvard has law, science, health science, all of which are equally good, but the Business School (Cleveland) is the most global. Similarly, for Cleveland, it has other health areas, (equally good) but they simply stand out in heart/cardiac departments. I have been privileged to study at Harvard from 2007-2009 and then I was in Cleveland in 2010, to address health issues. Two of the greatest and the best in the world.

I have always asked myself: why do some places become 'outstanding'? It is perhaps the same as saying: how do 'good' companies become 'great' companies? I watched Harvard and Cleveland closely to observe the greatness factor of these institutions. Yes, when you look at it closely, you see, very clearly, the systemic differences that must have been transplanted very early in their system, and continues to live on. This is always a challenge, and an area that keeps me engaged for many hours. How do you merge or balance the human and behavioural aspects with the system and mix it in such a manner that a new product, which is also unique, gets created? If you do this well enough, then perhaps, a 'good' organisation becomes 'great'.

The brand value that they build over years creates expectations that need to be met consistently. As I walked through the corridor of the Cleveland Clinic one morning, four volunteers along the way asked me whether I needed any help. I felt good. But they were doing this to everyone, day in and day out. From my hospital room, I could see the valet parking guys, running to collect the cars. I watched it every day. They never walked. If I see my car being picked up like that, I would surely like it. Salaried doctors with yearly contracts, all add up to the brand value of Cleveland Clinic.

It's a scenic place with lots of vineyards and hills around; it is also a cool place. But what stands out is the genuine concern of everyone in the clinic. It is aptly summarized by the statement made by the concierge at the InterContinental Cleveland when we checked in on the first day. He said, 'We don't like or enjoy when patients check in to our hotel, as they have their grim faces on, with the treatment in front of them. But we get aptly compensated with joy, when we see their smiling faces when they check out after being cured.'

Thank you, Cleveland Clinic. Thank you for this energy you have brought in my life.

MEDITATING AT BALI

This was something I have been waiting for years. I have always experimented with myself, and always tried to discover and do things that I have never done in my life. It gives me a high. For quite some time now, I have been really wanting to spend more hours with myself. There was a certain kind of pull within me. But I was not getting there. So, last November, I went to Bangalore for a retreat at Sri Sri Ravi Shankar's ashram for a five-day basic course, as they call it. I was not pulled by anything. I was simply trying to know myself a little more. It was good.

I met Guruji, and he told me to do the advanced course, and try and live in this environment more. That's all.

So, this time when the opportunity came, I grabbed it.

We were in Bali for six days for this advance meditation course. Out of the six days, three days we were in total silence. That was mind-boggling. This is something I did not know at all. My son, Romit, has spent 11 days in total solitude and silence. My respect for him went up, many times, after he did that. He also came back, a much cooler guy. But also for me, total silence was also good for me, as I persevered—not looking at anyone, not touching anyone, and just being in the environment with myself.

All through the day, there were many things to do as part of the course. They were all done together. 600 of us. It began with yoga at 5.30 a.m. in the morning, and ended with satsang, which continued till 10 p.m. During the course, you are totally involved in the process.

This whole experience was huge for me. There was a lot of serenity around. Lots of breathing exercises. The whole essence is to breathe in, that's the first thing you do after you are born, and breathe out, which is the last thing you will do. There are so many ways to conserve energy, and then deploy it meaningfully, so that you are fresh all the time.

I met some very interesting people. All of them were in a happy mood and relaxed. They surrendered themselves to the guru, living a happy life with minimum expectations from anyone.

The period in silence was initially a little tough, but then I did not need to talk. It was wonderful. So much of energy conserved. It felt good within. I did not even feel like talking at all. It was so much better to be in silence.

SWAMI JITATMANANDA: MY TORCHBEARER

On 21 December 2020, I got a message, which I knew was coming. Swami Jitatmananda passed away. One of the most revered monks of our times, yet highly controversial, I had the good fortune of being in touch with him for the past 18-20 years. During this period, he moved from Swami Vivekananda's birthplace (where I first met him while he held the position of Secretary there) to at least four more locations, before finally moving into Swami Vivekananda's home at Alambazar Math, where Vivekananda had set up Ramakrishna Mission, Belur. He was in-charge of Alam Bazar Math for a while, and then he was moved from the position of Secretary, in a single room with an office, where all the disciples used to come. He used to sit in the verandah on a couch at times. But whenever he used to talk to his disciples, Alambazar Math would be full to the brim. He used to narrate lovely stories, relating them in a lucid way and linking life's values to his stories.

I was never so keen on such things. I thought (wrongly though) that I didn't have time for it, as I was immersed in running my business. A few years with Jitatmananda made me realise that the path I had chosen was only to give direction to the youth, work will get done on its own. He used to tell me, 'All you need to do in Globsyn, is to stand in that long corridor of yours, wear a white dress, with your captivating smile and walk through. That's all, rest will happen on its own!' Almost twice a week, I used to get up early in the morning and drive to Alambazar Math, just to seek his wisdom. He was so positive. There are many stories I have collected during my acquaintance with him, but I remember one vividly. He gave me diksha and said, 'Whether I am qualified to give you diksha or not, your time to get diksha has come.' I can see it in your eyes. So, get ready to receive diksha. So, on the eventful day, in his math, he himself made all the preparations for me. Then, as he was lighting the matchstick for the agarbatti, his silk dress caught fire. Since it was silk, the fire really caught on to him rapidly. He was not bothered at all. Shrugging the fire with his hands, he said: 'Let me go and change my dress.' After that, he got up casually and walked slowly towards his bedroom.

I have witnessed this myself. This was divinity being displayed. He would come to my B-School campus with his music organ and sing with my students. Whenever he used to meet me, he used to say: 'You are meant to do much bigger things in life. Stay positive, always, and keep moving.' He used to praise me hugely in public, which was very embarrassing. But that was how he was. Whenever he used to meet his disciples, he would first make them eat and then listen to them. He told me, a poor man with an empty stomach can't absorb anything. First give him food to eat, then tell him how he should work.

In today's world, he was a very rare phenomenon for me.

DISCOVERY OF THE NEW WORLD IN 2019

The year 2019 started with a hospital ambulance picking me up in an aircraft, which brought me from JFK to Dubai, and me somehow managing to get into the ambulance from my wheelchair and being driven straight to a speciality hospital, where arrangements were already made. I was back home, a few days later, after an all-round check-up to confirm that it was only a femur fracture and nothing else. But that was not a small thing—there were multiple fractures. My inability to walk gave rise to the thought that life may never be the same again for me. I didn't believe it. So, I focused on my physiotherapy, which was done at my residence by two specialists from the hospital twice a day. Today, when I look back, I realise what an amazing recovery it was.

Those months were life-changing. I spent a lot of time with myself in the hospital bed in USA, and later in India; I kept thinking to myself, 'Where do I go from here?' Luckily for me, my sons, Rahul and Romit, responded with huge commitment and focus, given the huge responsibility ahead of them and no boss there to assist them on a day-to-day basis. Businesses started doing well. The cash flow got streamlined and a method, though incremental, was brought into my madness, and with the base being strong, there was no looking back. Both the AI business and Notiva in banks started moving with good operational performance. Our Business School was always steady. The American client responded very well, and the numbers grew, while I was watching it from the sidelines.

I had a serious chat with my sons and both were ready to grow. They just wanted to come back to me, once a day, for any eventuality, maybe for an hour only. So, that was the time I started looking inwards. Deep inside me, after what I have been through in

2018, and not to speak of my bypass surgery in 2010, I was coming to terms with myself. I started thinking that as long as my brain is intact, which I thought was very much in shape, I can do things; it beckoned an an inner yearning, and all that I had learnt during those Bhutan trips, when I started looking at myself, came back to me and I started seeing myself within me.

Quite frankly, though, I had started the Kalyani Foundation as my first foundation project; it was, I realised, perhaps to show my MBA students the value of 'giving', rather than anything else. So, being an NGO or doing a CSR project was a bit different from what I wanted to do—I felt like these were more institutional. So, I thought of acting on this urge of doing something that I had been experiencing for quite a while. To remain strong and focused, and genuinely make a difference in that part of the society that needed huge support.

It was altruistic, no doubt, but also touching a deep chord within me, evoking certain feelings and making 'touching human lives' our credo while accepting that every action had to, first and foremost, touch our lives as well. It had to be a very 'personal', deep-down act. I looked up at the evening sky and saw a few planes flying; I then asked, 'Is this what people call PHILANTHROPY?' I was hugely touched. I had recovered from my injury, and started my first post-surgery venture, based on my core internal thinking of philanthropy, and started looking at a subject very close to my heart—the informal sector, about which it is loosely said that you are paid for your skills only when you perform, and not otherwise. So, talent, skills, might not be in sync with getting a 'job', and thereby, a salary, which the middle-class people are so used to. Thus, your salary cheque doesn't get into your bank, work or no work, every month. You have to earn it. Tough call, isn't it? Young, semi-urban middle-class people felt the tussle between the heart and the head. So, it is completely market-driven, though you are paid only for your talent. I told myself that I want to look at this segment closely. I wanted to give economic stability to the youth of this performing sector, without disturbing the ecosystem.

SECTION THREE

MIDDLE-CLASS DILEMMA

I come from a middle-class Bengali family,
yet I explored beyond the set value system.
That's why I overcame my fears and said a big 'Yes' to everything!

THE POWER OF A BIG 'YES'

In 1995, when I was in New York, I remember an incident while presenting the concept of 'Infinity'—the intelligent building to be made in Kolkata, in the presence of the then Chief Minister of West Bengal, the late Jyoti Basu. Someone from the hall got up and said *'Yes'*. That person had his fist up in the air in joy. Interestingly, he was an American who loved India, and later when I met him (I didn't know him), he told me that India needed a model building like the one I had just proposed very badly.

That 'Yes' had indeed inspired me. Similarly, when I write my blogs, I do get feedback from those with academic interests like insightful blogs or other thought-provoking blogs, but never has anyone shown that same enthusiasm that I found in that American decades ago and that expression 'Yes'. My blogs are not meant for just good reading. They are written, from my heart, as a call to my inner soul. They are my spontaneous writings to communicate my feelings with my target audience, so that they feel equally enthusiastic and we can time travel together. That enthusiasm of 'Yes' is indeed needed.

As I go deeper into the minds and lives of people who do not have basic resources in life, I suddenly find there is a crowd there seeking publicity for social work. Political parties, the so-called CSR funders, some very good and strong NGOs are all very keen to communicate and make their presence felt. In India, no matter what you want to do, there will always be this crowd who will hog the limelight. My concept of 'one to many' for the poor needs a strong agency in the middle. Institutional philanthropy like the one I am doing for the young performing artistes via the Calcutta Broadway Health Insurance Card is important to connect with all strata of the society, especially the poor and needy in every sector. If you pick up the informal sector, most of them are vulnerable to changes in the socio-economic environment. Giving them the courage to come out strong and live their own life and making it happen is the key to social work.

In our society, there are plenty of highly-educated, extremely well-read men and women with decent exposure who could take the next step, but are not taking it. Yes, the next step will have logistics and administration issues, but if they don't take the next step, the participation will not happen. Just saying, sitting, listening, watching, reading, feeling, emoting with such causes is almost a waste of time, if some of you do not take the next step. I urge all of you who feel strongly about it to just go ahead and take the next step. In our generation, we have seen our parents going to temples and performing weekly pujas at home to purify their souls and for the well-being of the family. That is a generation gone. If you continue doing only that, you are going backwards. Today, we must take it to the next logical step and act on it. Just like the way I try to reach out to the society through my blogs, hoping to generate need-based solutions for those sections that are underprivileged and do not have access to the means that we have.

I keep searching for that bright inner soul that is inquisitive and will make the difference to his/her immediate environment. One who will speak with all the conviction and enthusiasm, and say a BIG YES!

CREATE AN EQUITABLE SOCIETY

I can only speak for myself, but I believe most of us with a similar background and experience might reach similar conclusions in life. Once you have invested all your time, energy and experience into your entrepreneurial journey over a large number of years, say 30+, you reach a stage in your life when you go through interesting observations about your own self, both intellectually and socially. Entrepreneurship drives you towards the welfare of the society you live in. By employing, training and developing people, even for your professional benefits, you are servicing the needs of the society to a large extent.

Then comes a point in time in our life when this urge goes beyond your direct professional work or assistance, and extends itself to areas very close to your heart through philanthropy. You get immense joy when you do that. On the intellectual front, your urge

and spirit to innovate continues. However, you might feel, and in my case I definitely did, the need to have others—friends and close relations—believe in you and your path; you might even want them to join you in your new journey. You feel stronger by doing so and together with such teamwork, your energy flourishes at a different level and pace, and you continue to innovate and be very happy. If you don't find anyone around with the right mix of chemistry, you might start getting plateaued, as your energy level dips.

Let us all hope that entrepreneurs in this knowledge economy find what they aspire for, and build for everyone an equitable society full of innovation and creation of intellectual properties, contributing to this world. I hope this happens.

REMEMBERING 'DEV SAHAB'

I liked everything about him. His style, his grace, his dressing sense, his naughty smile, his love for good-looking girls, everything. There was an inane purity about whatever he did. Even when he talked about his affairs and women in his life, he said those with so much grace, openness and class. He was an icon to me. Something, or someone, I wanted to become, not as a profession but as a persona. No one will call 'Dev Sahab' a Casanova. He was not one, but he was an admirer of beauty, or all things that are beautiful in this world.

When I grew older, I started liking his grace more than his style. But the interesting thing was that I was never ever thinking of doing what he was doing as a profession, i.e. becoming an actor. That never went through my mind at all. Interesting! This tells me that I was more influenced by who he was, and not by what he did. I remember that several years back, I was interviewed for a magazine about my work life and entrepreneurship. The journalist asked, 'What do you think constitutes an ideal entrepreneur or what are the elements of a successful professional leader in business?'

Responding to the question, I had said, 'If there was someone with a combination of Jamshedji Tata, Dhirubhai Ambani and Dev Anand, that would make an ideal leader. One represents social justice in business, other epitomises growth and Dev Sahab radiates vibrant positive energy.'

I had met him at a Delhi Press Club meet several years ago; back then Amitabh Bachchan had joined politics and someone asked Dev Sahab, 'When are you going to join politics?' He had said instantly, 'I will never join. It is too difficult to be a politician. You have to think only about the country from morning till evening. I can't do that as I have to follow my creative pursuits.' 'What is your actual age?' he had been asked. In response, he said that the answer would depend on who was asking the question.

I remember reading his book *Romancing with life* at one go in a Hong Kong hotel on a Sunday morning. His personality comes out clearly in the book.

I wanted him to come to Globsyn and address my students and share some of his positive energy with them. It didn't happen. I spoke to him on the phone. He picked up the phone and asked: 'Why do you want to invite me?' I told him our subjects are the same. I work for the development of youth, and you have to come. Unfortunately, that year his diary was full, and I missed him. But just talking to him on the phone made my day.

There was an energy that always radiated from him. I would be lying if I say that I was not influenced by his persona as I was growing up. Many of my friends talk about my energy in life, and work. I used to quietly smile, but somewhere Dev Sahab must have contributed.

IS WORK A PLEASURE? WHY NOT!

Are middle-class Bengali youths shy of working hard, as interpreted by the rest of India? Shall we topple the set statistics and mindset about our work culture and turn work into pleasure?

During my journey as an entrepreneur, which I believe was partly accidental and partly because of my need to be in control, I have often seen how naivety while running a business has landed me in trouble. However, ignorance has made me pay, dearly, to compensate for this. The desire or aspiration to make a difference in the society has pushed me into various avoidable situations.

Then, why did I keep doing it? Day after day, month after month, year after year, 14-16 hours a day, I am involved in doing something, which has given me all the things I have mentioned above, and in pretty decent numbers. Then why? My family is equally concerned about this issue, as it has perhaps borne the maximum pressure for all that has happened to me, good and not so good. Today, my wife is essentially concerned about my health and whether these 16 hours put a pressure on my health regime.

But we keep doing it—happily or not so happily; irrespective of whether we are having fun, or having difficulties, we still keep pegging. So, that is why I keep telling myself that if my work extends to my pleasure time, then work must be giving that pleasure, for me to forego everything else, and spend time on my work. I used to love going to movies, but these days, I don't. I love to travel, and I still

do, as my work takes me to different parts of the world. I enjoyed cricket all my life, and I still do, though there has been too much cricket these days, which has at times reduced the finer elements of the game, which I used to enjoy earlier. I used to enjoy being with friends, but today our meetings are limited.

It is very difficult for me to find friends who are just 'friends'. Even if they are, I find it difficult to converse beyond a point, as the vocabulary has become restricted unless you link it with cricket, or travel, or any such thing that I enjoy doing. Sometimes, I wonder why I can't have a friend whose interests are completely different from mine, or someone with whom I have nothing in common. We could still be very good friends, I think.

All these lead to a simple theory perhaps. If a politician's son joins politics, if a doctor's son studies medicine, if a cricketer wants to spend time playing cricket all his life, the same perhaps is true with entrepreneurs. We continue to develop ideas, and try to monetize them--not necessarily to make money only, but also to get that belief that your idea works. We continue to pursue opportunities relentlessly, even if it doesn't make too much sense at times. We do. We do all all of this because work to us is pleasure, and we are somewhere getting maximum enjoyment, fulfilment and happiness from it.

THE SUBTLE POWER OF THE MIDDLE-CLASS BENGALI WOMAN

Whenever I get a chance to write or talk about my mother, I feel energetic. My mother was an exceptional woman. She might have missed out on many small things, which she could perhaps teach us, but we never missed out on the bigger ones. One of them was to respect everyone you interact with, irrespective of their age or relation. When I was in school, I used to get phone calls at home from friends, mostly girls, but never ever had she asked me who was calling me. She would simply pass on the telephone to me and say, 'It's your call.' The onus was on me to tell her as to who had called, and not the other way around. The same thing used to happen for letters. Letters were big stuff, before the e-mail hit the scene, in our school days. There was a rule in our house—the letter/envelope had to be opened by the person to whom it had been addressed to, even if you knew who had written it.

Respecting people, dealing with people warmly, and continuously thinking about how you can keep making a difference in your immediate environment all the time—these were some of the key learnings of those days. Some of these traits I see in my sons, and I feel they must have inherited it from their grandma.

Today, I presume all mothers are getting remembered. It's a good thing. It creates discipline and social value for our kids to see and follow. There must be continuity in life. Only then, it is fun.

WHEN PASSION BECOMES CORPORATISED

My wife keeps asking this question to me time and again. 'I have always seen you enjoying what you do, and most of the things you have done so far have been by choice; then, why is it that you get tensed, worried, and stressed out with the same work that you enjoy doing?'

Paradoxical? I don't know. But somewhere what she says is true. There is an element of contradiction between doing something that you love doing and doing it big, commercially. Isn't it? A lot of people will not like the word commercially along with 'love doing', and I understand that. But what I meant was that if the platform is business, and the passion transforms itself into a corporate, then, this 'commercial' issue comes in, isn't it?

Yes, I am passionate about driving the youth of today through technology and new-generation alternative education, which is work-oriented. This passion has made me define what I called the Software Finishing School in 1996. Then, I did research and realised that most forms of education need it today. So, we created the Knowledge Finishing School System, a technology-based tool to help guide the youth.

But it became a big subject. It grew. Businesses grew. Money management came in. To push research and quality, you needed more money. The source of money was only passion, which was perhaps not able to generate that kind of money needed to corporatise and seize the opportunity. So, I started pushing the apple cart, as my source of money was only ONE.

Now, can you see how my wife's question turns relevant? There are other ways and means to resolve this issue, which I will not use. So, the financial system available in the initial days of growth includes banks, investors and the like, and of course the business you do. With these three avenues, you need to do everything—growth, research, investments, and hiring the best talent. So, you are constantly worrying, or feeling the pressure.

Today, when I look back at those days of contradiction, I feel it was all worth it. It was tough to sail through, but once you do, you are really and totally in control.

The Big Picture

There comes a time in everyone's life when you need to take big decisions. It could be your education, marriage, job and even your life as a whole. With the kind of middle-class family we had at home, in my case, most of the time, I was left to take those decisions myself, all by myself. But never ever had I faced a situation like what I faced this time, as it was about my life, my future, my health, and my family—all rolled into one, leading to a single decision point. There were easy points available with minimum interventions, or the BIG Ticket was available for me to take. What makes you decide on such major situations in life? The impact of such decisions on myself, my life, my family, my state of being, will have to be watched, but one thing is for sure. Having taken that decision, and gone through the process, I feel very strong within me. I am very relaxed and confident as a person and also way happier, to have been able to cross a huge self-actualization process within me. This is a great, great high for me. But at the same time, I am also confronted with the realities of the BIG Ticket decision in the interim, which has social attributes. I need to overcome them.

MY VIZAG DAYS

I have very fond memories of Vizag (Visakhapatnam). That was where I almost started my first job. I say almost as I did have one before that, but there's not much to talk about that. It was IOL (Indian Oxygen Limited), Visakhapatnam, that shaped me. I landed in Vizag with a trunk and a bedding, not knowing anything about the place. I was just 22 years old, thus, naive and innocent as I did not know much, and was yet to discover what I could do at work.

The language, Telugu, was like Greek to me. But I wanted to rent a place and went about seeing the places around my office. Very soon, I started my life there. This was a very eventful period in my life. I was alone initially, then my mother joined me. My Dad was with my elder brother. Within one year, I borrowed ₹2,500 from my dad to buy a second-hand Lambretta scooter, which used to start after seven kicks, and stopped running very often. I also did not have enough money to buy more than 2 litres of petrol at a time, so I used to run out of petrol very often.

I had a great boss—Mr Balagopalan. I have learnt so much from him including how you can be a perfect gentleman and command respect. He was fairly young and we started our work together in the coastal city in Andhra Pradesh. I was given a company jeep to drive and use. Within three years, it became quite easy to lead my life there. I bought a mobike, this time a new one. I had lots of friends, boys and girls, attended lots of parties and did well at work—life was on.

One of my close friends, Sohan, had a restaurant called Pink Elephant, and we used to all assemble at the restaurant for our evening sessions. I had a khata system, which means that I paid on a monthly basis, after getting my salary, and the restaurant had a bar license. I used to almost eat there every day. There was a 'Bong'

(Bengali) cook who used to cook special dishes for me, and it was all great fun.

Then suddenly, I got a severe attack of Amoebiasis. I was 25 years old that time. My parents came over, and the doctor said I needed timely, home-cooked food and a relaxed life. I was also told not to smoke cigarettes or drink alcohol by the doctor. That was the time when it had dawned on me that if this is where I had reached in my life, I should consider getting married and settle down. No one, including my mother, was prepared to accept that I was open for an arranged marriage. They kept saying, 'It's fine, but who is the girl? Let us talk to her parents.' I told them there are so many of them that you will lose count, you might as well do it yourself, and get one for me. During that time, I had developed a relationship with Deepak, who used to sell Kusum Products in Andhra Pradesh as an Area Manager. On one of his trips, Deepak brought his wife, Noton, along.

We hit it off immediately. Noton then started talking about getting a good girl for me to marry. That is how things started, and the rest is history. It was a very compelling period, so I will write about it separately, some other time. But Vizag, with its beaches, friends, mobikes and bachelorhood, was a great period in my life.

I thoroughly enjoyed it.

TO DAD WITH LOVE!

I remember him (my dad) as a stickler for right and wrong. He was disciplined and very clean, and willing to do anything to protest against any wrong-doing. He was also an able administrator. He retired as Joint Secretary, CSIR, Ministry of Science and Technology, Government of India. He had been one of the early employees of CSIR when it was formed in 1943-44, with Shanti Swarup Bhatnagar as the first Director General. I remember my dad telling us how proud he was to be working with Mr Bhatnagar.

My dad's passion was creative writing and acting on the stage. He involved himself in these forms of artistic pursuits as a hobby. As we grew, we saw dad in many avatars. Firstly, when we were young, he shifted his focus on us and wrote poems for us. He was the first person to translate English nursery rhymes into Bengali for us. This was called *Biliti Chhara*, this was in the 1960s. It was a runaway success. This book found place in almost every educated middle-class Bengali home, bought by young parents for their kids, and became very popular. We all grew up listening to the rhymes of:

Jack Jill dui jon, haath dhorey bhai bon...

My father's writings were growing in style and stature, and my brother and I were growing in that shadow, both physically and mentally. He kept writing historical, scientific, educational stories on great people, as well as verses/poems for young, school-going boys and girls. We grew up listening to his poems. He was proud to publish books—from *Sharodiya Chhara, Ghoom Bhanganee Chhara, Bigyaner Chhara, Chhoraate Ramayan* meant for children at first, and then *Gadadhar, Ma-Moni, Ek Je Chhilo Raja* that were primarily books about the life of great saints. These were few of his works. My dad also wrote a number of contemporary dramas, short stories, kabya sangeet and poems.

Looking back and seeing today's world through my dad's eyes, and then putting my cap on top of it, I find that this balancing of mind is a basic need in most of us. He had a strange mix of skills and talents—being a great administrator, social fighter and creative writer. This mix may be inherent in many of us. We keep adjusting and balancing ourselves—some use it as a stress buster, while others are more passionate about pursuing their creative journey to achieve happiness and bliss. Maybe, there is some confusion when you do both mid-career. Can you sustain both? I don't know. For me the proliferation of my creative instincts happened in two clear ways:

1. Developing our company strategies, brand positioning, transforming the culture of the organisation, and mixing work with some activities in my career days.

2. When you get less active professionally, then your inner talents, skills, creativity, which were suppressed due to work or business pressures, start emerging and take shape. Like my entire mind in the creative space, I have tried to capture my life's journey in my memoir *I Did It My Way*, then through my web portal www.bdgfoundation.org by communicating with the outside world through my blogs and stories, a host of my philanthropic work (through the Calcutta Broadway and Kalyani Foundation) and my startup investments via BDG Angels. This mix, I saw it in my dad. And I would like to give a lot of credit to him for this skill of mine, factoring the period and time. For me, as long as my thoughts can show directions to the middle-class youth and the aspiring entrepreneur, I will be happy.

I have always wondered whether my father was a better poet or a better administrator. People would say perhaps similar things about me, only time would tell. But one thing is for sure. My creative expressions and journey added a lot of value and became an extension of my active life through my intellect, and I will most certainly credit my dad for that.

Baba, Pronaam nio.

15 TAGORE PARK

I have many fond memories of Tagore Park. I was between 9-13 years old then. My dad was in the peak of his career, a very hardworking, conscientious person, and was very involved in his work. My mother was the most accomplished lady I have met in my life—she was immaculate, graceful and social. She had this charm in her because of which all of my father's friends, like Khokon Mama, Rathin Mama, Nemai Mama, used to come to our house after work to meet her and enjoy her company. She used to cook for all. She was the most popular 'Didi'.

She was also active in Mahila Samity, where she was the president. She was very strict with us about our studies, but used to encourage us for a lot of extracurricular activities. I was very keen on sports, always. She also used to love seeing movies. The good thing was that she always travelled to the movie hall in a taxi—this was a big bonus for us because my dad would never take a taxi and always wanted all of us to travel by bus. After movies, the buses were always very crowded.

15 Tagore Park, was artiste Mukul Dey's house, bought along with a parcel of land by the Government of India. My dad got this huge bungalow as an allotment to him. It was a big house with a playground, lawn, two outhouses and a building shaped like a summer cottage; there were big rooms and also a huge veranda. The good thing was that there was enough space to play cricket, which I loved. We had a whole enclosure for support staff and Bahadur and his wife used to stay there, apart from other domestic helps. Bahadur's job was to look after me. He used to take me to school, bring me back, help me with my games, etc. I still remember his face. A very nice guy. Every year in 15 Tagore Park, we had many parties and get-

togethers. My mother was a great host. Once we had a huge picnic for all writers, composers and famous literary people and they spent an entire day with us. There were about 60-70 of them. They were all dad's friends. My dad was very attached to children's literature and used to write poems for children, which were extremely well-written. He was an extremely talented person. Then, family members from my famous 'Mamar Bari' (my maternal uncle's house), which we were very attached to, used to assemble at least once a year for a get-together and picnic.

Over 100 of them used to come to visit us. We used to have a huge photo session in the afternoon, and that used to go into the albums. My neighbours in 15 Tagore Park were Rana, Raja, Debu, Anjan, Barsha and Khokon. Debu's dad was a very senior businessman. He had a car and a driver; and he always looked very serious. He used to wear a gown at home. I was a little bit in awe of him. I thought he must be a 'boro lok' ('big man') with lots of money. Rana and Raja's dad was great fun. He was very loving and keen on sports. He used to play with us on Sundays. Both his sons were good in sports. I remember he had long nails. I did not understand why. Anjan was a little older than us but was a leader. We used to listen to him. He used to stay close to the main road. Khokon and Barsha were brother and sister and their mother was a very charming lady; but they also made us feel like we were a little too well-off. So, we were a little scared of them. But she was otherwise a very pleasant lady. Barsha was the only girl in the group.

Everybody fell for her. She was petite, good-looking and smart. We felt she could be a little too good for all of us. She used to give attention to me and Debu, a little more than the others, but I never got to find out more from her about her feelings. All these friends of mine are lost today. At times, when I pass through South City, which was where Jay Engineering was earlier, and the entry of 15 Tagore Park was on the other side of the road, opposite to which the wall of Jay Engineering started, I feel like getting down from the car and walking around that place, and may be, that is how I will suddenly meet one of them. I still see the jewellery shop on the road—Sarat Jewellery Works—where my mother used to go. It is still there. I thought, one day, I will go and ask them. But I have never done that. They must have heard about me, but whether they have been able to place me, I don't know. By writing this note about 15 Tagore Park, I am going back to those days of joy and having an opportunity to acknowledge people who played a role in my life. This is my way of expressing my gratitude to them.

SECTION FOUR

COVID-19 TEACHINGS

The world has indeed changed post COVID-19 and instead of fearing and getting depressed, let's take life lessons from this pandemic and its aftermath. Only adaptation to a crisis will sail us through. Think and answer: has lockdown taught you how to self-assess?

USE YOUR TIME TO GENERATE CLARITY WITHIN YOURSELF

There are many of us who have worked, built families, and engaged in various social/cultural activities for well over 30 years. These are people in the age group of 55 and above. We have seen it all, as they say or 'nothing' as some would comment. My question to them is: how are you spending your time during this lockdown period? Let's make it more difficult. Let us talk about people who are not actively involved in business or professional work now, but their mobility has been affected by this pandemic for months. What are they doing? What have they done so far during the lockdown days? Let them go back to the third week of March, and share a day-by-day rundown, till today, and take stock of their activities and their contribution to the society—offering help with family chores, which they never did earlier, pursuing hobbies, reading books, writing, practising or learning new skills, etc. Can you check yourself on that? I mean, check only on yourself. What did you do?

And once you start questioning, you will get very interesting answers. I respect privacy. So, you need not say or write that in public. First, simply note it down somewhere and then go through it and see how much of those you would consider as waste of time and money on a normal day in your life? On the contrary, you may also care to check what new ideas you have generated, new thoughts you have created, the new ways you have discovered to live life, how many people have you made happier, how much of clarity you have been able to generate within yourself because of the time you got etc. Did you use this time available to generate clarity?

I am just provoking you to do an audit of your time management in an unprecedented situation like this—which you have already spent and won't be able to go back to. It's a huge learning.

How much of clarity have you been able to generate within yourself...

SERVICING REDEFINED POST COVID-19

COVID-19 has indeed shaken all industries across the globe, bringing in huge strategic re-thinking to adjust to a new world, where a virus has been wreaking havoc—not just on humans and their health but also on the economy. Many individuals, who apparently had built themselves during the pre-Covid era, are finding themselves lost. There is a huge adjustment that everyone is going through within themselves. But the fundamental point is that no one knows where it is headed to. Businesses, in particular 'retail' or most of the service businesses for that matter, are not able to figure out the direction as the future is so unpredictable.

I keep talking to entrepreneurs and I find they are at a loss primarily as both buyers and sellers are confused about their way ahead. A lot of waiting and posturing is going on. 'I am fine, I don't know about you' is a general theme. For example, these days we are seeing a lot of music videos, Facebook Live, but perhaps none of them (including the artistes) have thought through what this could mean—whether, or how much, they are impacting their own professional fees, as people or channels, as the case maybe, and their audiences get used to this online forum. What will happen to their skills offline, something that is their core competency and helps them earn? But they also need to

be visible in these tough days. You need organisational thinking here. Any individual, however talented they are, can do very little if they are not supported by organisational inputs.

Take for example the cricketers and the BCCI. Can they survive on their own? Don't they need BCCI for their survival? Similarly, those in performing arts need to rethink their strategy. How will they flourish their art forms during these trying times and even later? As for corporates and their products and services, they need to work out distribution models differently to reach their customers. Sure, web-based operations look ideal but may not be enough for all segments, especially where there is innovation involved and where touch and feel are important before buying the product or services offered.

Even higher education has gone through a perceptible change. Web meetings, webinars, web-based classrooms are already being implemented. I just want to make education players aware that the

customers are very unaware currently. They don't know how education products in the new regime could succeed, or how their end customers, both retail and institutional, will behave going forward. So, for the next one year at least this will continue. However, clients will hire people who will understand the market, absorb and be dynamic to this change. So, the recruiters/corporates and the higher education institutes must deliberate and discuss what the end user needs and wants, and how these can be delivered, to be productive, profitable and impactful to their students in these challenging situations. The bottom line is, however, clear—adapting to technology vehicles is the key. Understanding the changing needs of clients is more crucial.

THE WORLD IS WIDE OPEN

In our life so far, we are governed by certain norms and governance rules that is prevalent in the society, and our parents/guardians direct us as they have seen through their earlier generations and so on. We do claim, however, in recent times that we are very open, liberal, free with our family, kids, friends etc. But somehow the rules of the society still govern in every household with certain amount of relaxation and freedom, which we call ourselves as being 'liberal'. But we still follow the same growing-up norms that come in a cycle—of school, college, university, job, marriage, family and kids.

But what about today? Everything is genuinely and literally open and is beyond anyone's control—so much so that even shaking hands with a friend, whom you are meeting after a while, is not a 'done' thing. We do not know timings for anything. We do not know when colleges will open, whether going to work is safe enough, visiting malls is safe? Cinema halls are a non-starter still.

One invisible demon has made 7 billion people in this universe get up and take note in this modern, high technology world of ours. If you have loads of money, or if you don't, it's the same. The virus doesn't discriminate. But this changed 'new normal' is taking a toll on mental health. People are becoming reactive at home; with too much of nothing, we are perhaps losing our balance at times. Let us have faith and belief in our own skills and happiness, and live in that space as much as we can. Maybe, then we might find some solace. Too much of openness is impossible to manage. Many of us have realised that within ourselves. Maybe this will help build a new form of sanity within us.

ENJOY SELF-DEVELOPMENT!

Due to the onslaught of COVID-19, we were all trying to understand and fall into a pattern of living with the pandemic—avoid infections by taking necessary precautions (even if at times some of us end up ignoring them, mostly because of lack of understanding of the whole situation). Many friends and acquaintances have been infected by the virus and recovered, and there are many who have escaped infection so far. Fatalities are still below 2 per cent. The question today, I am raising in your mind is: what did COVID-19 show us?

It meant many things to many people, but what did it mean to you? Is there a common thread that connects all of us across the board, especially the younger generation? The answer, I feel, is 'Yes'. I will pick up only one of the many areas wherein, I feel, many of us have had an opportunity to practice and excel. That to my mind is SELF-DEVELOPMENT. Many of you know that self-development is a continuous, ongoing process and it needs to be understood, learnt and practiced, as part of our ongoing life and its commitments. All of us need self-development and we have been through it, in some way or the other, but COVID-19 has provided us with that space, time and energy to focus on it and work on ourselves.

How do you practice self-development? First, you need to strictly identify where you are in life today? Then, where you want to be? You would have noticed, many of your well-wishers, would have identified your areas of self-development. This must have been identified by you, directly or indirectly, several times. You also happen to know your own developmental needs and limitations. Put all these together, come up with a process of how to go about it, and then list it out and be ready to start. This MUST be done by you, all by yourself, and in a relaxed way.

Many of us are entrepreneurs, or in corporate business, creative sciences, performing arts, consultancy-advisory, operations etc. Your first set of identification is based on your background and experience. This has to be done by YOU. Identification of self-development needs is half the battle won. Once you cross that, you are now ready to execute your plan.

HAS THE WORLD ORDER CHANGED POST COVID-19?

USA with over 325 million, China with 140 billion, India with over 130 billion population has had unique but quite disturbing data of late, with regard to COVID-19 and the world order. These three countries alone account for over 40 per cent of the world's population. So, whatever happens in these countries will impact a large chunk of humanity, to say the least. The Wuhan-originated virus and the human tragedy that followed with allegations of China suppressing reports of mass deaths and infections, the disturbing saga of over 12 billion migration workers moving from one part to the other part of India due to lockdown, the 'black man' George Floyd killing in Minneapolis, USA, have left all of us in a huge sense of disbelief and bewilderment.

As if the severity of the pandemic and the economic crisis that followed was not enough, these incidents have demonstrated on the streets how the world is being treated these days. Is it Nature's own way of saying 'Enough is enough'? Now, think of your people and their welfare, build your country, bring in more compassion and love in whatever you do and think spiritually if you have to address issues confronting the world.

In 2014, in one of his now famous speeches, Bill Gates had predicted that the next world war will not be fought by pressing the nuclear button, but by an invisible virus that will be all pervasive. Today, we are progressing very clearly and surely to the post-Nostradamus phase of our lives, into a different world where perhaps spirituality will rule the roost and not just the fear of a religious order.

What does it mean for us? We all know by now, when the atomic war was being fought fiercely, how an innocuous concept like 'non-violence' captured the mind and hearts of many in the world. On a similar note, will a new definition of spirituality emerge, where love, care, compassion, inner belief and thinking will give rise to FREEDOM and throw away our anger, hatred, pettiness and claustrophobic and narrow-minded parochial thinking, which has encaged us as 'slaves'. The fear of something unknown, which though temporary, is restricting the passage of liberty and freedom.

But not for too long though. We will keep fighting against negativities and try to open up a bold, new world of love and freedom. Trust me, it will happen someday. It has to happen, for all of us to survive, and for the human race to keep going.

A NEW SOCIETY POST COVID-19

It's a very funny time that Nature is taking us through. First, there is no end in sight to COVID-19 and now we have a huge cyclonic storm, Amphan, sweeping our coasts, and set to hit our city anytime in the afternoon. Interestingly, I have reached that stage of my life wherein thinking, planning and developing the future for the self has become a myth. But humans are very funny creatures. It's like the amber light in a traffic signal. Praying that I should get through, let the guy behind me see the red light. This is how we think even about work, development and everything.

We keep telling ourselves 'live by the day' or 'live in the present', but do we practice that? Or can we? We drift away to hope or despair, whatever our state of being at that point is, and start day-dreaming. It reminds me of the classic Bengali play in which I performed the lead role, some 40 years back. It was named *Jodi Aami, Kintoo Aami*. Translated, it means something like *If I was, but I am*. Our self, or even selfish orientation, doesn't keep us in that zone always.

Ironically, in management circles and in society, as we were speaking of the efficacy of working together, working in groups, in teams, back to community development etc. in came COVID-19 and declared: 'Social distancing, please!' This was a direct contradiction to the concept of team-building and working together in close missions. Such is life. But we will re-group. I am confident that all of us will work out some mechanisms, and a time will come again when we shall go to the theatres, watch movies (not Netflix), and attend wedding receptions, seminars and the like. Once our work pattern, or our money earning pattern, changes, community development changes. Some will struggle, some will adjust and some will be in total bewilderment.

So, nobody has the answer today, we only have questions. A majority of us are just floating and seeing where and how we can fit in—at work, as family, as professionals, as themselves, in this new emerging society. Let the search begin...

NEW NORMAL EVEN IN HUMAN RELATIONSHIPS

Our relationships will undoubtedly change post COVID-19. India will get affected quite significantly. Ever since our birth, when we were toddlers, 'warmth' signifies a certain amount of touch, though not necessarily so. But most of our relationships develop through close contact—face-to-face conversations, hugs, shaking hands, close looks. This is something that we call 'body language'. Mind you, knowingly or maybe unknowingly, we grow in our lives this way. So, unless you are a toddler today, who will be

trained in a new way, most of us are victims of our so-called 'relationship' dynamics, which hugely depends on people with whom you have spent years of your life.

If we have not met someone, but have heard about him, we tend to say: 'I don't know him, but let's go and meet him.' We don't normally say: 'I don't know him, we can always send an e-mail to him.' In today's world, contacts like e-mails and WhatsApp might establish a basic virtual contact, but it is normally followed by a quick meet, and then handshakes, hugs etc. But the three basic norms of the COVID-19 protocol are: Clean your hands, practise social distancing, and wear masks. If this is the new normal, then, it is taking us away from our 'normal' relationship matrix. I am not even talking of expressing love, affection etc. I am still much behind on all those. Just imagine, what if the new world order makes us follow the COVID-19 protocol throughout our life. Then, what happens? Many reading this will say, 'Oh, come on! This is only till a vaccine comes.' So, all of us, are always looking at these protocols, very temporarily. Just suppose, they are not. Even with vaccines, there are many stages. First, it should be available, then it should be distributed to the common man, we should be able to get it easily and all these are practically still a distant dream for the common man, especially for the middle-aged people. But until COVID-19 vaccines become available in the same way as, say, an antibiotic, life will be different; and I want to ask a more fundamental question to all of you.

Can you cope with that life, as your new normal? Will virtual relationships be as intense as contact relationships? Will the strength and intensity of bonding, love and care change in the new times? Shall we turn more 'cold' in human relationships? Will it have a permanent impact in our society, in terms of relationships? If not, well and good.

DISCIPLINED DUBAI IN THE TIMES OF COVID-19

On 2 September 2020, we finally made our family trip to Dubai, where our son Romit (Sunny) lives. Since then, it has been a completely different life for all of us. Life is almost normal here. You can socialize, go to malls, attend meetings, go to office, as everybody is strictly following the norms related to COVID-19 (masking up, social distancing, cleaning hands etc.) It is heartening to see everyone and I repeat EVERYONE following the norms. Some people say that it is because of the strict implementation. Whatever it is, it is being done for everyone's safety only and so, everyone should follow this anyway.

That done, life becomes so much easier for everyone after that. I have been engaging in a lot of work after coming here. Both my sons are here, and we meet very often. We have regular strategy sessions, new investment opportunities and the like. My granddaughter, Mishka, has started going to school here and an almost normal life is back.

Everyone is finding their own way of settling down in their lives, based on the situations in front of them, and what they can do or not do. We all feel, if this has to be a part of our lives, let's work out our schedule around it. I am very happy to see how people, as a society, are disciplined to follow the norms and they are also seeing the benefits of the same.

New business, no matter what, is an issue, as the market dynamics keep changing, and we are always trying to see what will work on both the sides. Interesting!

NEW CREATIVE ORDER: STRUCTURED PASSION

In the past seven years or so, several times I have been asked this question: 'Why do you need to do more work-wise? You have done enough, now you should relax and enjoy your life. Your sons are running your businesses well, so what is the worry?'

I have not been able to communicate (though I am otherwise a good communicator) that what they call 'work' is pleasure for me.

When as a creative and passionate person, you have tried to bring your creations into the world, and benefitted the society, for all your life, and it has, in turn, given you immense happiness, making money out of them comes at the very end of it. This is something I have failed to convince my well-wishers. Ironically, these well-wishers are my closest people. My family, direct relatives, who supposedly know me well. How little we know, isn't it?

I was just reading a foreword by Sandip Ray about his father in the book *Short Takes*. In it, Ray has said that his father, the genius Late Satyajit Ray, did most of his creations himself—he bought the big scrolls of paper, mounted them on the wall and started creating and expressing himself. All over the world, you give your thoughts and someone else creates it, but Ray created his thoughts, mostly by himself. All of us got to see what was in his mind as he expressed it through his brush and/or his writing. Passionate people like us have this inner desire and hunger to talk to their clients directly, through their own work. When the work gets accepted and the clients express huge happiness and fulfilment of his requirements/needs, reaching many people who then propagate to make it popular in society, so that more people can enjoy and participate in that journey—that's when the creator has a sense of satisfaction, not before that.

This whole process is like generating a huge amount of energy within the system. Energy is always regenerated, recreated and goes on and on. So, the passion to create gives it a stimulus to transcend in the society, giving joy to millions. The creator is then satisfied. This is a self-generated form of expression, which through the creator's urge of passion, generates a huge amount of energy, which then creates the end product, whatever that might be. The creator keeps generating this energy, which is re-cycled and passionately delivered to the society through the creator's vision.

There is definitely an end or objective of the creator, which is

to benefit the society and people at large. His creations enhance knowledge, experience and understanding within the society, thus making the society and its people richer internally. That's how entrepreneurs fill in the 'gaps' in the society and people benefit immensely. So, there is nothing called 'being tired' of doing this or that, or even saying that 'you have done enough, now you can relax'. The creator will always say, 'I am relaxing.'

This is the world I have lived in the past 35 years. Isn't this exciting? I continue to do so every day of my life. Luckily, there is no retirement age for entrepreneurs and they can keep creating, whenever they see a gap in the society that they want to fill. Maybe, finally I have answered my well-wishers—that I have not done enough, I am not tired and I am enjoying my life as long as I keep creating, and bridging the gaps in our society, passionately through my creations.

So, Passion, Energy, Creativity, in a structured manner is what we (entrepreneurs) have been generating day in and day out for years; and we will continue to do so, as long as the society lives and grows, and gaps get created with growth. It is STRUCTURED PASSION that creates the architecture of modern-day advancements in the society. Satyajit Ray was no exception, though he took it to a level that is very difficult to emulate, let alone sustain.

EPILOGUE

I have tried all my life to motivate the youth, for in them I find the future, the energy to build something new, and fresh ideas that will help the world. Hence, the sole purpose of my 'Blog Book' was to help them in their journey by sharing my real-life experiences—struggles, challenges and successes—that I have scripted during my entrepreneurial journey.

During different phases of my life, I have written down these blogs and I still keep writing for the innumerable young minds across the world who have been following my blogs since many years. This book is a comprehensive answer to their queries and thoughts. From spiritual healing to hardcore corporate challenges, my blogs cover all aspects needed to inspire young minds to tread a path for a better tomorrow.

So all the best readers! Hope you find your dreams and positive thoughts through my blogs and reach the pinnacles of success in whatever you do!